DORSET ESSAYS

Llewelyn Powys

DORSET ESSAYS

With 16 black and white photographs by Ann Clarke

REDCLIFFE
Bristol

First published in 1935

This enlarged selection of essays first published in 1983 by Redcliffe Press Ltd, 14 Dowry Square, Bristol 8.

ISBN 0 905459 53 9

Photoset and printed in Great Britain by Photobooks (Bristol) Ltd, Barton Manor, St. Philips, Bristol BS2 0RN

CONTENTS

CONTENTS

LIST OF ILLUSTRATIONS

THE WHITE NOSE

WHEN I first lived in one of the coastguard cottages on the top of the White Nose I was in considerable doubt as to my correct address. As a child I had been taught to refer to the cliff as the White Nore; on the other hand the gate of the coastguard station through which I passed every day presented my eyes with the words White Nothe; while the people of Chaldon Herring were all of them confident that I was living at White Nose. It was this last judgement which eventually won emphatic confirmation from the late Mr. Thomas Hardy, who said: "Of course it is White Nose, it always has been called White Nose. You can see if you look that the cliff is shaped like a nose. It is like the Duke of Wellington's nose." From that afternoon I have been careful to use the local name.

Although White Nose approaches an altitude of six hundred feet, it is not as high as Golden Cap, but both its position and its "countenance" render it the noblest of all the Dorset headlands. This proud sea headland, conspicuous from the Esplanade at Weymouth, is a promontory of many mysteries. It would take a boy longer than a summer's holiday to explore all the secret Robin-Hood-retreats of the under-cliff, the giddy ledges and castle rocks to be found in that strip of broken ground which extends as far as the blue slopes of shale where the "Holworth volcano" once burned. In the winter this under-cliff is entirely deserted, a forest abandoned to the partridge, to the raven, and to the red fox. In the early summer, when there are forget-me-nots in the turf by the cliff's edge, minute as the bright chips of enamel in a brooch, a pair of shiftless magpies translated into dutiful fowls of troth, give themselves to the exacting task of rearing young in a clumsy "nitch" of prick-thorns. This happens during that fugitive period when the voice of the cuckoo is audible far out over the waves of Weymouth Bay, and larks are singing all day long high up above open strategic foot-square platforms where zigzag figured adders lie curled for hour after hour in a voluptuous torpor warming their close dry scales.

Often I have walked through these strange landslide glades in the moonlight, and never have I looked upon patches of grass that have suggested more certainly old Celtic imaginings, so that I could almost fancy I heard "the bridle's ring" of the fairy court riding by through the fresh seaside air which the scent of wild privet renders so softly sweet on an evening in early June.

There are groves grown thick with ancient elders, whose skeleton branches are white as marrow bones, groves where the old ballad witch might well hold her step-children under a glamour, the boy as a "laily worm" and Lady Masery as "a mackerel of the sea":

"An' every Saturday at noon
The mackerel comes to me,
An' she takes my laily head
An' lays it on her knee,
She kaims it wi' a siller kaim,
An' washes 't in the sea."

Not only is medieval lore fostered by this majestic headland, its slanting levels are decorated with centaury, that beautiful pink flower shaped like a star, called centaury because its medicinal properties were first discovered by Chiron, the centaur, when he was schooling the heroes under the rowan-trees of the Thessalian glade. This small flower, with good justice, puts us in mind of ancient Greece and for the discerning the White Nose is perhaps more classical than medieval in spirit as it rises against the blue sky, so light, so marble, so well-proportioned.

At low tide it is possible after a scramble over rocks to round the dark base of the bastion until the curving bay to the eastward is visible. This chaste gull-haunted stretch of the Dorset coast can be reached by climbing down a hidden and very dangerous smuggler's path at Middle Bottom. This is an undertaking, however, only possible to one who still enjoys the sure foot of youth and a head unaffrighted by dizzy drops. Otherwise to reach the beach a man must swim.

From the shutter rock, just round the corner of the point, the deep water stretches for only a few yards. Once across this the adventurer is rewarded. Here under the dense weight of White Nose is a very ancient and little-known cave. It requires no great imagination to believe that clear-seen Dorset is the lost island of Ogygia and this cave the hollow cave where the sea nymph Calypso held Ulysses as paramour for seven long years, perhaps the very cave where he so often received refreshment in the half moonlight; begetting his two sons, Nansithous and Nousinous, and where his heart yearned for high-born Penelope, his dear mortal love, and for the small rocky goat-grazing island, his native land. Out onto the beach he would go each morning, disturbing the patient cormorants, "whose business is in the waters, to tread fisherman fashion the shelving shingle, his thoughts in far Ithaca." All day long he would speak out his trouble to his own great heart, until at the fall of another evening, passing weary, he would return to the couch of the beautiful sea maiden of the braided tresses, "an unwilling lover by the side of a willing lady."

If the White Nose hides strange secrets at its foot where the wild lavender blows, certainly it is not possible for a man to stand on its wind-swept forehead and remain dead in spirit. To the west across gentle meadows, across the sunset pools of Lodmoor, it is possible to make out St. Catherine's Chapel raised like a goblin's thick thumb over the down, and further, the cliffs of Devon, and further still, on an exceptionally clear evening, Start Point. To the east lie, one behind the other, Swyre Head, Flowers Barrow, and St. Aldhelm's Head—the eternal hills of Dorset.

The White Nose is so tall that it is no uncommon thing to stand in full sunshine and look down upon clouds lying, fold upon fold, as far as Portland Bill, as though a bed were preparing for a cloud-gathering god. In stormy weather, when the purple shadows are scudding across the Bay, it is the best place in the world from which to see a rainbow, a widespread arch with one ethereal end resting upon the crested waves, and the other upon the vexèd grass of the downs, a triumphant heavenly arch with colours as dazzling as the feathers of birds in the Caribbean islands, as bright as scales of fish in Caribbean seas, and compelling even the most sorrow-laden to lift up their hearts in gratitude for the rich guerdon of the visible world.

THE DURDLE DOOR

HOW individual a feature of Dorset coast is the great oolite archway situated westward of Lulworth Cove known as the Durdle Door. The Pulpit Rock at Portland Bill, and the Old Harry Rock between Studland and Swanage, are not more dear to natives of Dorset. The Durdle Door is sometimes called the Barn Door, and the homeliness of this title accords well with its shape, for, viewed either from sea or land, this broken cliff has the simple look that often belongs to the entrances of old out-buildings of agrarian husbandry, entrances wide enough to admit a broad-beamed country waggon burdened high with corn sheafs. The appearance of this rugged, firmly standing portal of the open sea suggests an ancient human building, the weathering it has received differing little from the weathering that has fallen upon the square belfry tower of Sherborne Abbey, upon the vaulted ashlar roof of St. Catherine's Chapel at Abbotsbury, or upon the mellowed masonry of such venerable secular habitations as Wolfeton House and Melcombe Bingham.

I recall only once having know the ravens to select the Durdle Door for their February nesting. They reared their brood on its precipitous southern wall that year, their insatiable black chicks incessantly calling for their meat across a mackerel sea. It is a remarkable fact that the celebrated promontory has never been favoured by mating gulls. Are they perhaps aware that it is possible for a daring boy to climb along the whole length of the Durdle Door; whereas to the westward Bats Head offers innumerable marble white ledges, inaccessible without the aid of ropes?

On a summer's morning the Durdle Door Bay can present a very harmless and tranquil appearance. At intervals curling waves break upon its shingle, waves not high enough to overset a child's toy boat. Samphire, flower of St. Peter, that has managed to root itself in the rough interstices of the huge sea gate, seems as naturally placed as are patches of mistletoe upon an apple tree bowed down with age. The sea between the Durdle Door and the Blind Cow Rock suggests, when the sun is shining, the blue transparency of the Mediterranean, reminding a lover of Capri of the water surrounding the grottoes on the southern side of the romantic Neapolitan island. Bathers, however, should be careful. Only strong and experienced swimmers should ever venture through the arch into the open sea, for at certain times of the year dangerous currents may be encountered. My father used always to warn us about this, and in my own time I can remember several visitors being drowned. The safest bathing place is to the east of the Durdle Door in St. Oswald's Bay. Here the Man-of-War-Rock performs the service of a strong breakwater, and it is a happy sight in August to observe human beings basking like seals upon its slippery expanses, thick-matted with sea-weed, subjects of the king who might belong to a blither civilisation than it has been our fortune to know. It is possible, indeed, that Phoenician traders, familiar with the gaiety of classical holidays, may have disported themselves on these very boulders—for does not the great down that towers over it take its name, Tout, from the Phoenician deity, Theut, proving beyond all disputation that this section of the coast was well known to those adventurous traffickers of antiquity? Though from the writings of Tacitus it can be inferred that Caractacus died at Rome, there has always existed a persistent rumour amongst the shepherds and fishermen of the Lulworth district that the barrow so ceremoniously crowning Hamboro Tout marks the true burying place of this famous chieftain. A wayfarer who takes the trouble to climb up to this tumulus will be richly rewarded. Its position affords one of the finest views in south Dorset. It was on the summit of Hamboro Tout that Farmer Diffy built his bonfire for the Jubilee of King George, the most impressive Beltane fire seen on that gala night south of the Frome.

From Nore to Tout
Never a flout,
As foxes are free

In earths by the sea,
Each lass and lad
With love is glad.

Squire and farmer
*Plowman, crow starver,**
As merry as weasels
In a bed of teasels,
As frolic as stoats
In a field of oats.

Of the world of convention
I pray you no mention,
Tingling with malice
From cottage to palace
It can change overnight
Wrong into right.†

I well remember the occasion when I first saw the Durdle Door. We children had come by the Lulworth steamer from Weymouth under the care of our nurse Emily. I could not have been ten years old. Walking up the street from the Cove we stood spell-bound by the spectacle of a large cat outside the door of one of the cottages. This cat was being treated as if it were a dog. It had a leather collar about its neck and a chain attached to a kennel. The animal looked so content and well cared for that my sister put out her hand to stroke it, immediately receiving a savage scratch.

Thirty years afterwards I was refreshing myself with a cup of tea in one of the same cottages and mentioned the incident. My hostess, Mrs. Miller, going into her private parlour, brought back a photograph of the very animal. It was to her that the cat had belonged and the accident had happened in the very garden where I was now enjoying my tea.

A strange glamour had always surrounded my childhood recollections of this visit to the Durdle Door, and the sight of this imposing shadow of "Fluff," so solidly presented in an

* A crow-starver in old Dorset is a rook boy hired to keep the crows from the corn.
† This essay was written in the early spring of 1935.

enlarged photograph of the period, connected in a most reassuring way the very real present with the radiance of those past memories. Animals come and go, long processions of human races—Saxons, Britons, Iberians—come and go. Merely to possess marrow bones is to possess material treacherously designed for perishing. Matter itself is not immune from these terrifying atomic transmutations. Yes, even the Durdle Door, that ancient hatchway of resistant limestone, honoured by generations of Dorset men and women, has little permanence. It forms but an image of relative durability destined in the passing of a few millenniums to be consumed by its contact with wild waves.

THE FOSSIL FOREST

IF a visitor to Lulworth crosses to the eastern side of the Cove, and climbing up the slope of the cliff, follows one of the numerous tracks that wind through the gorse, he will soon be within a hundred yards of the Fossil Forest.

The famous platform lies halfway down the cliff and is easily accessible to all but the very young and the very old. It is a wild place of congregated rocks, blown bare by sea winds, washed bare by sea frit, and parched bare by sea sunshine. Even in midwinter on a cloudless day one can sit here as if it were the month of August, so absolutely is the gallery sheltered from the north by the shelving "broken beds," and beyond by the huge mass of Bindon Hill. In summer the platform's heat is Mediterranean in its intensity, and as one looks from the sky-blue sea at the sea-blue sky it is easy to imagine oneself on one of those dizzy ledges that surround the Siren Island of Capri.

Nor is the Fossil Forest entirely devoid of vegetation. In crumbling crevices, and on patches of dry turf, there are two plants that grow prosperously—samphire and thrift. Both are plants of character, the first with its thick succulent stalks tartly smelling of the watery ocean; and the second, lovely as the old-fashioned garden pink, with a habit of growth so closely attached to the coast that it will wither and die rather than suffer transplantation for as short a distance as fifty yards inland.

Few people take the trouble to climb down to the Fossil Forest and it is likely that the wayfarer will be alone here with rocks, sea, and sun for hour after hour. Even if such an adventurer should know nothing of geology his attention could not but be arrested by the petrified boles of the ancient trees. Lucretius, perhaps the most inspired of the old Latin poets, in a famous passage explains the appearance of the Earth's living creatures in the following manner: "For neither can living animals have fallen from the sky . . . it remains that rightly has the earth won the name of Mother since out of the earth all things are produced. . . . For much heat and moisture abounded then in the fields, thereby, wherever a suitable spot or place was afforded, there grew up wombs clinging to the earth by their roots." It was out of these natural wombs of fecundity, so he believed, that animals first sprang in their various forms. And truly, when one examines these extraordinary Cycadean stools they do suggest to the imagination immense matrices, so that, recalling the great poet's imagination, one can well conceive haughty unicorn and crooked-jawed boar leaping from such centres, new born into life! On account of the odd shapes that the encrusting carbonate of lime has given to them the fossilised concentric cavities that are uncovered by quarry-men on Portland are called "crow's nests," less informed workmen of the old days having concluded that these fossil nests had at one time or another fallen out of the branches of the trees of stone which the excavations on the island so frequently expose.

The petrified matter enveloping the base of these trunks is sometimes formed with circular ridges and depressions, which, so it has been conjectured, were originally caused by the ripples of the shallow water in which the coniferous timber was growing.

The massive boles that we look at in the Fossil Forest belong to the Jurassic Age. For this reason geological authorities calculate that since the period of the flourishing of these trees at least eight million years have gone by. In truth these fossils are of so hoar an antiquity that during the age in which they grew the ancestral forerunner of men was no more formidable than a little marsupial, resembling the jumping rat, whose eager preoccupation it was to keep out of the way of the invincible reptiles who were then the lords of the earth. Even within the span of the Jurassic Age there went by periods of endless time with the salt ocean making vast encroachments upon the land and then again receding—encroaching and receding, receding and again encroaching. In lagoons filled sometimes with salt water, sometimes with brackish water, sometimes with fresh water, the dinosaurs took their pastime, dread, hairless dragons, abroad in the steaming rain showers, in the blaze of midday, and somnolent under the moon.

Around fern-like growths, palmettos and trees of the coniferæ family, clouds of grey insects quivered and danced; but when the sun uprose from the ocean wastes, beyond where St. Aldhelm's Head now stands, there were no birds with tremulous madrigals to hold the dawn under an enchantment. In their stead across the Lodmoor-like sunsets of those tropical evenings pterodactyls winged their way—flying lizards with the jaw bones of their horrid heads well fitted with jagged teeth and the span of their bat-like membrane wings measuring several feet from hooked finger to hooked finger. As yet there were no butterflies to flicker over the surfaces of the lukewarm pools or to settle with damask wings opening and shutting upon the crinkled bark of half-submerged logs. Everywhere through the wide levels of the shining sea the ichthyosaurus dived, more vicious and more voracious than is shag or cormorant to-day sharking for the flesh of fish on the lew side of the Blind Cow Rock.

Not long ago I was present when the shoulder blade of a plesiosaurus, found by Miss Woolsey and now in the County Museum at Dorchester, was dug out of the clay at Ringstead. It was an impressive relic of that time which outstretched man's power of comprehension. The newt with chilled belly and the dry sultry adder are but puny representatives of those cold-blooded, cold eyed sauria whose dynasties remained for so long unchallenged. Those huge creatures upon whose plated flanks soft feather or glossy hair never grew, these pitiless gigantic lizards unprovided with udders with which to suckle their slippery young, in due time gave place, according to the inexorable ordinance of nature, to creatures whose blood by a novel dispensation preserved an even temperature however inclement the climate.

Æons upon æons followed, and then once more a strange instability troubled the earth's crust and the Forest Downs were lifted up and serrated mountain-ranges wrenched themselves across the continents, and presently man, separating himself from the other animals, raised out of the dust his tragic head of laughter and of woe.

It is possible to-day to rest at full length in a sarcophagus-stone at the Fossil Forest. Long ago this massive shell surrounded the wood of a fallen specimen of one of these primæval trees. Surely in such a coffin out of eternity the most frivolous mind should find release from time-imprisoning illusions, and exulting in the free gift of life, grow strong to contemplate all problems with a scrupulous intellectual integrity undismayed by the thought of death.

BATS HEAD

TO anyone with good eyesight, the great promontory of Bats Head can be seen from Weymouth Esplanade. It projects into the sea a few miles to the west of Lulworth, and far below on each side of its perpendicular chalk face lie two deserted beaches, the one to the east falling away to the Durdle Door, and the other to the west extending as far as White Nose. It is a remarkable headland. On afternoons of the wildest weather a man may rest here in tranquillity, some peculiarity in the structure of the cliff causing the rushing gales to cast themselves straight up from its sheer walls, so that the crest of the headland remains in an absolute calm. Seated on this halcyon ledge it is possible to observe in peace the riot of the sea-coast below; to look down upon great black-backed gulls flying in wide circles along the margins of the breaking waves; or to watch at close quarters the cormorants pressing their bodies in mid-air against the wind, their black necks tilted upwards.

There is something outlandish and forbidding about cormorants. Milton must have recognised a turpitude in them or he would never have made Satan select this particular disguise for entering the tropical acres of the Garden of Eden. How obstinate an egoism have these gluttonous sea-crows! Wherever they are it is the same, whether settling upon the water like mallards, or in groups upon a rock stretching out their wings like black fans to dry, or when, with the deliberation characteristic of them, they sweep forward through a marine twilight to their selected roosting places. What secret mandate are they obeying on such occasions? At whose word do these impious birds direct their unerring flight over the face of the waters? Bewick says that in some parts of the world men make leather jackets out of cormorant skins. How admirable to be defended against wind and sleet by a jerkin of cormorant pelts! In the reign of Charles I the position of Master of the

Cormorants was a much-prized office—and no wonder. Who could aspire to a more impressive and singular title? Imagine the curtains of the royal audience-room thrown open and the doorkeeper announcing the entrance of so carefree a functionary!

In sophisticated subtlety the cormorant is not to be compared with the guillemots. There is a narrow ledge halfway up Bats Head where the guillemots have congregated in the nesting season for time out of mind. Here they will stand for hours upon their black webbed feet, nodding like punctilious mandarins at each other, until embarrassed by their own self-conscious manners they dive off from their chalky platform, and with their odd mechanical flight circle down to the sea. With us the return of the guillemots each spring is a recording place in the advance of the seasons. "The foolish guillemots have come," we say, as others speak of the first arrival of the swallows. What a commentary it is upon the brutal insensitiveness of man that these refined birds should have won for themselves the epithet of foolish; foolish, forsooth, because "in their piety" they will remain upon their eggs until fishermen can catch them and wring their necks.

It is, of course, the herring-gulls which through spring, summer, autumn, and winter, make up the real bird-population of these cliffs. It is their hungry call that first breaks the religious stillness of the winter dawn, vexing the waking dreams of the countrymen with their wild insistent crying, before even the red glow is to be seen through the lowest branches of the naked hedge. It is these birds which may also be seen walking on the grasslands in November, white as a flock of faery-tale geese, or rising up suddenly out of rain-soaked stubble, like a shower of snow in a child's glass ball. At this time of the year they come in from the restless sea, from the ridged weed-drifting margins of the shingle, to glut their insatiable appetites upon the lowly victuals of the soil. Up into the cloudy winter sky they mount with their free strong flight, a flight so different from that of a chapel of starlings suddenly flushed and close-clustering as a swarm of bees.

How the knavish cliff-jackdaws are for ever striving to

imitate the balance, the aerial poise, of these incomparable white birds, and yet for all their javeline dartings, they can never escape the ordained limitations of their being.

The White Nose ravens seem entirely to disregard all other fowl. Their dark shadows cross and recross the sloping shoulders of the downs, but they are always flying alone, the male and the female, with solitary, mutual love. In February, when they prepare for their first clutch of eggs, they are self-sufficient, and in mid-winter, when they come in over Swyre Head after a morning's scavenging on the Chesil Beach, it is the same. What a massive self-absorption is suggested by the croak of a raven, as it disturbs the stillness of a Sunday afternoon far up above the gorse and carline thistles. No wonder to primitive minds this harsh utterance seemed to conceal hidden meanings, dark occult messages, decrees of a dolorous Fate. There is only one pair of ravens nesting now at White Nose. Each autumn they drive their offspring westward. These unnatural battles usually take place above the undercliff, towards Ringstead. I was once told by the late Mr. Hardy that when he was a boy it was a common thing to see village people bless themselves as these birds flew above the thatched roofs of their cottages far inland, so that seventy or eighty years ago ravens must have been less rare in Dorset than now.

Aloof though the White Nose ravens are there is one bird that breaks in upon their proud isolation. For some obscure reason the heavy, dark flight of these giants of the air is exasperating to peregrine falcons. The war between the ravens and these hawks is a perennial as the traditional contest between pigmies and cranes. A peregrine falcon will pester a raven in its flight for several miles together, soaring high up above it and then with a deadly swoop darting downwards. I have seen them knock feathers out of the raven's body, but never do serious harm, and it is astonishing how the great bird knows when to turn upon its back in mid-air at the very instant when in its downward rush the peregrine is ready to strike. If the peregrine's attacks become too insistent the raven will fly to the ground, and whenever it is driven to this extremity the hawk will molest it no further, appreciating, I suppose, how formidable a weapon is its heavy, black, hollow beak—a true Saxon battle-axe!

Men have sought for the secret of life in temples and in cathedrals. They have worshipped in moonlit groves and before the sacrificial stones of monolithic circles. With closed lips and shut eyes they have waited and listened for God in corn-fields and vineyards. I think there are few places more fitted for such moods of religious receptivity than is this undisturbed sea-cliff. Here for thousands upon thousands of years the sunlight and the sea and the masterless winds have held tryst together, and nature, under the sway of so mighty a trinity, shows without reluctance her hidden moods, moods violent and material, moods of a severe and chaste beauty, and moods that are full of a deep and tremulous earth-poetry.

THE GRAVE OF WILLIAM BARNES

THOUGH I recognise it as a form of primitive ancestor-worship, I always desire to visit the graves of great men who have brought enlightenment to the human mind. I would have liked very much, for instance, to have seen the huge stone at Delphi, so often referred to by Greek writers, upon which were to be read the awe-inspiring words "Here lies the body of Dionysus."

In my own country I have been fortunate enough to visit the graves of three remarkable poets whose years edged the span of my own days: the grave of Matthew Arnold in the village of Laleham, not a stone's throw from his beloved Thames; the grave of Edward Fitzgerald, the last of the Epicureans, who keeps his "morningless and unawakening sleep" in the heavy clay of Suffolk; and the grave of William Barnes, who might almost be described as the "last of the believers," and who is buried in the little yard that surrounds the church of Winterborne Came.

For many years I was foolish enough to mistake Whitcombe Church for Came Church. I even on one occasion explored its green enclosure in search of the poet's grave, never imagining that there could be a church even nearer to the road-side Rectory.

It was three years ago in the month of June that I left the Dorchester train at the little platform of Monkton and began my belated pilgrimage to the true burying-place. The summer's day was redolent of the old man's genius. The fat meadowlands on my right, golden with a myriad buttercup globes, seemed to render completely plausible the simplicities of his faith. The "shrouded" elm trees and low-boughed oak trees appeared like ancient bards blessing the opulent pastures; with calm assurance prophesying peace to unending generations. My very bones responded in loyalty to the unassuming poetry of this good Church of England clergyman, who, though holding stoutly by the ancient pieties, never failed to oppose with all his might the oppressions of men "hardy and industrious to support Tyrannic power."

No poet in all English literature has done more to reveal the quality of homely village days as they follow, one after the other, against their background of the fugitive, recurring seasons. These bucolic poems, so innocent and so sturdy, instruct us how to become accessible to the wonder latent in every mode of natural existence, teach us to be grateful for the privilege of life on its simplest terms, with firm purpose and serene minds, to face our inevitable lot of sorrow and death.

I found the graveyard of Came far more secluded than that of either Laleham or Boulge. From this acre of hallowed ground I could see English meadows lying swart in the blaze of noon exactly as they had done for centuries upon centuries. They had looked like this when "King Gearge wer in Dorset, an' show'd his round feace." They had looked like this when the maidens of Protestant Taunton had put on their white frocks to welcome the Duke of Monmouth. They had looked like this when Spanish galleons of Philip's Armada had been visible driving before the wind from Portland Bill to St. Aldhelm's Head all one stormy dog-day. "He blew and they were scattered." They cannot have appeared very different when John Lack-land was hunting tall red stags over the bog-cotton moors of Purbeck Island, or even during the Junes of that dim century which saw King Lear at war with the turbulent elements on Egdon Heath.

Approaching the church past the home cottages of "Herrenston" I noticed a date clearly indented upon the lead of an old, rose-mantled water-pump. I cannot remember for certain, but I think the recorded year was 1817. At any rate it marked a date long before William Barnes' incumbency. I could not but think how often his eyes must have rested upon these numbers known to him as well as the finger-polished latches of our doors are known to us, as, for twenty-five years, with his black satchel, he went to and fro for the performance of his offices in the small church. Often enough he must in winter-time have passed this pump when the ears of the boys sliding on the duck-pond were "so red's a cock's cwom," the ruts on the high road full of cat's ice, and the "huffling" wind caused swinging twig icicles to tinkle as he came down the avenue to the white gate. Often he must have passed it when the primroses were out in the copses and the gold of the celandines in the ditches beginning to show silver, and he would see little Dorchester girls looking for white violets on the sheltered bank opposite the turnpike house of Max Gate. Often he must have passed it in summer-time when

"A-vleen drough
The leafy trees, the whoa'se gookoo
Do zing to mowers that do zet
Their zives on end, and stan' to whet."

and again in the autumn, in October, November, when the rooks "wi' sheenen wings" gathered from the cold hungry plough-lands as early as half-past three for their noisy congregated flights to the King Rookery in tree-sheltered Warmwell. Many an aged body in his parish who remembered the French Revolution and the preaching of John Wesley, this old-fashioned English priest must have fortified in the hour of death, absolving their sins with the wide allowances natural to one who had no love for "hard words."

Already William Barnes is but a legendary figure to the majority of Dorset people. Only folk of sixty years and over could possibly remember him walking through the streets of Dorchester in his eighteenth-century dress. Those who knew him well, the quick of his time, have long since been gathered to their fathers under the uneven grass of town and village churchyard.

The lettering on the Celtic cross that strangely enough was selected to mark the grave of this learned scholar of "eald Saxon," is already filled up with moss.

I remember being told by my mother that when I was a baby she carried me from Rothesay House to Came Rectory that I might receive the old poet's blessing, and I find as the years pass that my mutinous thoughts are more reconciled to acknowledge the wisdom of a certain prose passage from the works of this simple "interpreter" of the fairest county in England: "I had been working in my garden. The sun was just below the horizon and the dew was already on the small green walks bordered by sweet-smelling roses and carnations. The stillness of the evening was broken only by the whistling of a blackbird. I sat down on a rude seat I had formed beneath an old tree and, as I thought of the fruits and plants that were ripening around me, I exclaimed to myself: 'How happy if they knew it, are they that till the ground.'"

A BRONZE AGE VALLEY

IF a wayfarer walking by the cliff path from Lulworth Cove to the White Nose pauses when he has climbed to the top of Swyre Head he will be in a position for scanning every feature of the valley that lies between him and Bats Head, the next high promontory to the westward. The valley is a wide sunny acreage snugly sheltered from the north by the ridge of the downs along which runs the grassy gypsy track locally known as the Roman Road. Chainey Bottom, for so the Bottom is called, taking its name from an iron chain which was once hung over the cliffs by the coastguards and still may be used by active people, is likely enough to be, except for rabbits, utterly deserted. Half-way up its steep slopes a dead elder tree is occasionally to be seen—a bare skeleton whose paralysed back and crooked arms have been washed to their marrow by many a south-western gale.

Herring gulls cross and recross the Bottom, flying in from the sea, hungry for their plough-land food and then again returning to fish, settle themselves upon the waves a little distance from the foreshore, like a flock of halcyons buoyant and at peace. A raven may also shadow for a moment the clumps of stinking-iris, the sage, and the fine rough grasses that, during the hot summer, become as yellow as the grass upon an African plain. It appears that in the Bronze Age, and probably later, this undisturbed valley was closely inhabited by man. When the sun is low in the sky, either in the morning or in the evening, the ridges of the cultivated plots of these seaside dwellers can distinctly be seen. There are many such dividing "baulks" discernible, and though the sizes of the plots they enclose vary, they are usually considerably larger than the amount of ground that today would be rented for an allotment in Dorchester or Weymouth.

Towards the lower end of the valley there is a well. Tradition connects this with the activities of the smugglers, and I have heard some of the older fishermen of Lulworth say that as boys they remember the remains of a false bottom protruding from the well's sides—a false bottom that had been constructed for confounding the excisemen.

My brother, Mr. A. R. Powys, was inclined to believe that this well, though undoubtedly useful to the smugglers, had been originally dug by men of the Bronze Age. He also suggested that the oddly symmetrical circles of flint that still are conspicuous in the valley, marked the sites of the village huts, built about with rough walls of flints sunk possibly a little below the surface level and roofed with boughs and grass. When the walls of these huts eventually collapsed the flints that tumbled into the saucer-like floor fell so closely congregated as to defy the encroachments of the surrounding grass, each advance that it made in the wet mild winter being cancelled by the action of the next summer's sun upon a practically soilless area, so that even after the passing of two thousand years the old position of the dwellings remains today as clearly defined as ever. The winding trackway used by these men for entering the valley is also to be traced working its way on to the settlement from the north-eastern corner. My attention was first directed to this remarkable seaside hamlet by Mr. Salzman, the historian, who was for a short time a neighbour of mine at the old coastguard station on White Nose. He brought back one afternoon several fragments of Bronze Age pottery that the rabbits had scraped out. It is possible that there may have been some erosion of the cliffs during the last two millenniums, but it cannot have been very considerable and Durdle Door and Bats Head, those two sturdy deep sea bulwarks of the valley, must have stood out much as they do today. The principal landmarks on the surrounding downs all have to do with the lives of these men of old time, either with their daily occupations, or with their deaths, or with their religion.

Dominating the immediate landscape is the circular earthwork marked on the ordnance maps as the "Pound." It is an enclosure, the broad round earth rampart of which would still be valuable for purposes of defence. When seen from a distance it suggests a miniature Maiden Castle, so prominently do its green sides, crowned with gorse and elder, rise up amid the acres of waving corn. Some years ago I examined it with Mr. Prideaux, the late curator of Dorchester Museum. It was his opinion that the Pound might possibly have served as a primitive temple, and surely to lie in the centre of this august circle constitutes a religious experience. With the clouds silently moving across the firmament a man's nature would be gross indeed if it were not initiated into the very mood of these Dorset hills, so patient and so enduring in their strong simplicity. Here indeed is a place for the weighing of the power of the soul, alone, and, as it were, balanced beneath the heavens in one of those scales of ultimate judgement so dear to Egyptian mythology.

The conspicuous barrow called Woodwards barrow, standing at the top of "Tumbledown," a field of flints and plovers, is separated from the Pound by only a few hundred yards. This barrow was built by the same people. Let our minds revert to the afternoon when the mourners returned to Chainey Bottom leaving the corpse of their chief to pass its first night in a chalky grave. Several days must have been required to prepare this impressive tumulus for interment. The surface soil within a large circumference was probably loosened with deerhorn picks, and having been collected in heaps with the help of the shoulder blades of the same animal was conveyed by means of skins and wicker baskets to the centre where the great mound was being piled up. When finished it probably appeared twice as high as it is today, its present subsidence being due to the continual attrition of the mound through the usages of twenty-five centuries.

In the sight of God it is but a day since these men and women were living in Chainey Bottom, watching anxiously to see how their crops of barley were beginning to sprout, or to "chimp," as we say in Dorset. On early spring mornings the Island of Portland across the azure blue of Weymouth Bay must have appeared much as we ourselves see it.

In every direction the higher ground above the valley is even now thick with the tools that these people flaked into carefully designed shapes—"thunder stones," or elf shot, as they were called in the middle ages—in many cases never since picked up by human fingers! But the dwellers in Chainey Bottom were not only agriculturists, hunters, and fishermen, they were stock men also, driving the cattle down to water in the Winfrith, Lulworth, and Ringstead valleys; and herding them at night into the Pound—a place easily guarded by a few resolute drovers; resembling as it does the native cattle bomas I used to see in Africa. As with us the sun would come up over the Purbeck hills and go down over Wyke, or at midsummer further west still behind the heather-covered Blackdown hills, where game would be almost as plentiful as in the great forest of Selwood below High Stoy.

Essentially the lives of these old inhabitants of Chainey Bottom were not very different from our own. They were stirred by the same emotions, by the same hopes and fears. As we love our wives and our children so did they love their wives and their children, and as the more sanguine amongst us eagerly entertain the hope of a life after death so also did these men, skin-covered and squatting on their haunches. Often they must have looked up at the Milky Way above the waters of the Channel, and, even as we do, for brief intervals have forgotten their day-by-day ordinary life, vaguely apprehending with rude imaginations the deep poetic mystery of existence.

For a moment, perhaps, as the soft winds, blowing across from the Chesil Beach, touched their foreheads, the real would seem less real, and the well-known objects of their every-day use—odd-shaped fish hooks and earthenware milking pots that they were constantly handling—would lose suddenly their insistent actuality, and the happy life of the sheltered valley, with the evening voices of children mingling with the wild talk of the herring gulls, would take to itself, for a moment, a dream-like quality, unstable as the surface of a vast tidal river that bears all before it, on and on, to a limitless and eternal ocean.

From Bats Head, looking towards Durdle Door.

Bats Head from the east.

GIPSIES

LITHE as a weasel, shy as a fox, slinking, slouching, with his jointed gib-cat limbs superbly oiled by the hand of nature, a gipsy youth appeared from behind the Merlin thorn-tree. My brother and I had left the White Nose cliff, and were walking towards the grassy track that runs parallel with the coast-line between Poxwell and Lulworth, known locally as the Roman Road. The boy was under twenty and a perfect specimen of his race. He had the shining eyes of a God and his teeth were as flashing bright as those of a naked, spear-bearing Masai. As we approached he stood aside, carelessly treading upon the wayside bluebells with his clumsy shoes, the "uppers" of which had been split for the sake of comfort. With his slanting gaze turned from us he uttered a sing-song sentence. I concluded that he was begging. We stopped and asked him to repeat what he was saying. He was inquiring whether we had seen a "burra worra." I could not imagine what wild animal he meant to denote by this name. When, however, he pointed out just where he had seen the creature disappear through the gorse-bushes, I decided that he had caught sight of a badger, for I knew badgers did cross here in the early morning on their way to the undercliff.

"He must have meant a badger," I said to my brother as we walked away. "He saw nothing," was my brother's answer. "That odd word has probably earned him repeated pieces of silver. Very likely it is an extremely old word of theirs. It may very well have been practised upon Sir William Temple when he stepped out of his park to whistle for his secretary. No "burra worra' has ever existed; it is a name invented to arrest the attention of preoccupied country gentlemen in preparation for a more serious exploitation of their good nature."

That evening I spent several hours with the gipsies. Whenever I get a chance I always sit with them over their camp-fires. As usual they were ingratiating enough, saying just what they thought would please me most. From the old woman leaning against a log whittling sticks for clothes-pegs to the dusky urchin sprawling in the dirt before the black tent, where was truth to be found? I mean that relative truth that serves our turn on earth.

There were five or six hobbled horses grazing some fifty yards away, grazing in a place where, because of a wide gap, it would be inevitable for them sooner or later to stray into Farmer Cobb's clover. At intervals the boy I had met with my brother John in the morning would get up and disappear into the darkness, ostensibly to see that all was in order, actually to make sure that the nags were not losing their opportunity.

As I sat on by the fire I came more and more to appreciate the wild wisdom natural to this nomadic people. Never has a true Romany been duped into substituting the false values of civilisation for the true values of life. They know what they know. Centuries of oppression, centuries of persecution have never persuaded them "to scorn and abhor the shining of the sun"; never for a moment have they hesitated in a choice between settled domesticity and their passion for a *safari* life. We may well go to the gipsies for instruction. More than ever are we disposed to gauge the success of our lives foolishly. These sun-tanned Bedouins of our heaths and commons can show us a happier plan. They cannot be seduced by the artificial pleasures of urban life. Their spirits would wilt, their whole life-illusion be destroyed were they to lose direct contact with sunlight, with moonlight, with clouds, rain, sleet, hail, snow. Their sensuality is the sensuality of cats. It extends all over their bodies, over the whole surface of their brown pelts. *Carpe diem*. They live for the moment, casually, accidentally, like rats, with a snatch here and a gnaw there, satiety to-day and hunger to-morrow.

When one considers all that this race has suffered since it first migrated from the east one realises how strong an appeal Nature must have for her true children. I suppose the Jews, with their extraordinary vitality and racial consciousness, might have succeeded in keeping themselves apart under such conditions, but certainly no other people would have done so.

These "diddikis," as we call them in Dorset, for all their slippery dealings, are close to truth. We sophisticate existence. The old mother told me she had spent fifty Christmasses in the quarry over by Moreton. "We be terribly fond of thik place for Christmassing." In November, she told me, they travelled in Somerset. "The mistletoe be best in they orchards, down by Yeovil and Taunton ways."

With the smell of burning wood, the smell of trodden grass, the smell of human bodies, mediæval in its rankness, and with these wrinkled walnut faces lit up by firelight, by starlight, it was impossible not to respond to the poetry of their days. I have never been able to look at gipsies without a dim feeling of nostalgia. This strong fascination they exercise may well be explained by atavistic memories, taking our spirits back to wide Aryan plains, to vast periods of unrecorded human life. "They wandered in the wilderness in a solitary way, they found no city to dwell in." Always I feel a sense of loss when I see them come trailing through the streets of Weymouth, of Wareham, of Dorchester. How enviable is their detachment from the crowd. They are untouched by those senseless anxieties that perplex the rest of us. To observe their feckless loitering is to feel spiritually refreshed, as though, after all, we had but to take half a dozen steps, to be away with the raggle taggle gipsies:

> "O come with me, says Johnnie Faa;
> O come with me, my dearie,
> For I vow and I swear by my ashen stave
> That your lord shall naw mair come near ye."

Hunger, thirst, love, and liberty, they have no other cares. To see a young townsman on a pavement, energetic in body, spruce in dress, and time-imprisoned in mind, and to contrast him with one of these loiterers reclining gracefully at the curb, relaxed, nonchalant, *content to be alive*, is to receive a lesson as to wisdom and unwisdom. The preconceptions of the former are rigid and absolute, of the latter lozel, relative. The clerk's life-estimates have to do with gain and worldly prosperity; the gipsy's life-estimates hark back to an age when these man-made material cupidities were still unknown, and when consciousness was confined within the bounds of one's own peripheral sun-warmed skin and was so accepted by the religious senses.

It was some five hundred years ago that the gipsy tribes first began to appear in Europe. It has been suggested that they were original Arabs who had acted as spies for the crusaders and who migrated westward to avoid the wrath of the victorious Saracens; others affirm, and this is the theory approved of by scholars, that they are the descendants of a refugee people who fled from Northern India at the time of Tamerlane's conquests. All over Europe they spread, the men arrogant, intractable, and given to thieving; the women versed in fortune-telling and the occult arts. There are many who believe that playing-cards were introduced into the Western world by gipsy women for purposes of divination by sortilege. Some of the men take to horse jobbing; others make a feint at being tinkers or coppersmiths, but for the most part they live by picking and stealing. It is this weakness, perhaps, that has roused against them such implacable hatred. In France they are known as Bohemians, in Spain as Gitanos, in Germany as Tartars. Civilisation has from time to time become restive under the burden of these parasites, and, like the rhinoceros when tick-birds settle on its back, it has raged and plunged, though its harsh protests have availed little.

In the reign of Elizabeth it has been estimated that there were ten thousand gipsies in England alone. An early seventeenth-century writer alludes to them in the following manner. "This kind of people about a hundred years ago, beganne to gather an head . . . and this as I am informed was the beginning. Certain Egyptians, banished their country (belike not for their good condition) arrived heere in England, who, for quaint tricks and devices not known here at that time among us, were esteemed and had in great admiration in so much that many of our English conycatchers joined with them and in time learned their crafty cozening."

The Statute book of Henry VIII refers to them as "an outlandish people, calling themselves Egyptians, using no craft no feat of merchandise, who have come into the realm and gone from shire to shire and place to place in great company and used great subtle and crafty means to deceive the people."

Wherever they have gone it has been the same, society has turned fiercely upon them, upon these turnpike sneak-thieves who are as adroit to whisk away a goose at Michaelmas as to snatch a smock from a cottage hedge in the spring-time. In Scotland the Privy Council passed a law ordering all "vagabonds, sorcerers, commonly called Egyptians, to pass forth out of the realm and never to return to the same under pain of death." Numbers of gipsies were actually hanged in Edinburgh. They were regarded as outlaws, beyond the pale of human compassion, an inferior kind of species less deserving of respect than animals, the men to be killed, the women branded, or drowned. As George Borrow wrote "the gibbets of England groaned and creaked beneath the weight of gipsy carcasses." It was not until the reign of George III that they became punishable only under the Vagrant Act.

Still the gipsies survive, live on in their old hereditary way:

> "The dingy tents are pitch'd; the fires
> Give to the wind their wavering spires;
> In dark knots crouch round the wild flame
> Their children, as when first they came."

When we consider our present industrial, mechanical, practical age, it is indeed wonderful that a sight of these primitive wanderers should even yet be vouchsafed to us, glimpses of these mysterious and ancient Ishmaelites, crossing our shining macadam roads with desert dust upon their sandals.

Do gipsies appeal perhaps to something incorrigibly antinomian in all of our natures so that we find it unsettling to our acquired docilities to meet in a woodland glade a people who have never acknowledged social obligations, who have been consistently indifferent to ethical systems, who have won the freedom from convention that we secretly crave, and, who, more than any of us, may be said to belong to the great many-breasted earth-mother?

It is amusing to remember that it was the gipsies themselves who first named themselves gipsies, with a very characteristic "burra worra" lie introducing themselves into Europe as "Counts of Litell Egypt." In our time they are in more danger of being squeezed out of existence than ever before. Benevolent landlords who are eccentric enough to shelter them are not as common as they once were. I know of many a chalk-pit, of many a lane from which they have been excluded. Squires, farmers, householders, police, combine to harry them. Motor-cars ravish their unnoticed byways, their hidden haunts; yet see how conservative these ranges are in their tastes and habits! Their women pass us by in sluttish beggar rags, and yet what sparkling bangles, what glittering jewels, what Asiatic finery! Like magpies they love what is bright, and like the Phœnix they survive the fires of destruction. Wherever they are, romance is! In a village in Somerset there is a gravestone put up by an aged gipsy, named Isaac Jowles, to the memory of his octogenarian wife; the old rogue has rendered his very egoism poetic:

> "Here lies Merrily Jowles
> A beauty bright
> She left Isaac Jowles
> Her heart's delight."

Down the centuries they have come, their hands against every man and every man's hands against them, a true people of the Pharaohs trusting in the sun, treacherous and mysterious.

A week after our meeting with the gipsy boy I saw smoke rising from behind the Merlin tree. Next morning I was out before dawn walking in the direction of the Roman Road. Nobody was stirring so I sat down behind a gorse-bush and waited in the half light. Presently the summer sun came up over the island of Purbeck. Its rays fell level with a myriad grasses. From barrow, thorn, and fence, long horizontal shadows lay across the dew-cool ground of the downs. The gorse was in bloom and the bluebells were fully out by the side of the track. Gold and blue, blue and gold. The sun was golden, the sky was blue; the sun was golden, the sea was blue. Everywhere larks were in the air and already there was a linnet with rosy breast, balancing itself upon a prickly twig. I heard a movement, the flaps of one of the tents was held apart up. A small girl showed herself. She could not have been more than thirteen years old, but never have I seen a look of such enchantment, of such rapture, upon a human face. Holding the canvas away from her elf locks she looked out upon the uplands as they stretched away towards St. Aldhelm's Head, fold behind fold. Perhaps this "black Indian" had been fretting all the winter in the slums of Southampton and had forgotten what Dorset was like in the pride of a morning in spring, had forgotten the beauty of the wild earth that was her inheritance.

HERBERT PARKER

IT is ten years since I returned home to England to live in one of the coastguard cottages at the top of White Nose. White Nose is an isolated place even in the summer months, but in the autumn and winter it is as desolate and lonely a headland as any to be found between Poole and Lyme Regis. The cries of the gulls at dawn, the husky barking of the foxes at twilight, the howling of the November gales—all conspire to put a modicum of good sense into a man's head: and one of the most valuable lessons learned is the importance of appreciating people, not on account of their rank and still less on account of their wealth, but for such personal qualities as honesty of mind, soundness of character, generosity of heart.

If I except the Ringstead fishermen, the neighbour I saw most of during my stay at White Nose was a man named Herbert Parker. He was born at the village of Osmington, and the world that he knew, though roofed by infinity, had for its friendly ramparts the sheltering chalk downs of South Dorset. With a famous line of the poet Virgil in his head William Barnes once exclaimed: "How happy, if they knew it, are they that till the ground." Mr. Parker was a farm-labourer who proved the truth of this scrap of ancient wisdom. He was the possessor of the following simple blessings, blessings that so often form the foundation of fortunate days. His disposition was by nature genial; until his last disastrous illness his health was invariably sound; and his marriage with an indulgent and capable housewife, equally gay in cornfield, cheese loft, or by fireside, had been rewarded by the birth of seven reliable and likely children.

This unostentatious family lives in one of the cottages in the Holworth Valley. Behind these cottages there is a spinney where violets and kingcups begin to show themselves at that uncertain time of the year when hailstones still fall from heaven like showers of daisy heads, and when the fingers of Saturday-morning children, for all the dancing sunshine, feel too numb and cold to gather the pussy willows. With the strengthening of the sun the wide pasture on the other side of the stile provides the earliest cowslips, short of stalk at first but tall by the end of April, and visible a long way off above the bright dairy grass. Each May nightingales nest in this small withy bed, the male bird arriving a few days before the female, to sing through the spring nights madrigals of desperate yearning for his brown companion, astray perhaps in her migratory flight above an endless acreage of restless sea waves.

Amid such country sights and sounds were the uneventful years of this honourable man's life spent. One after another, slowly, evenly, his meritorious days passed into oblivion. He was always good with his horses, and many an hour of a winter evening would he spend in the stables, his lantern hung on a rusty iron peg, currycombing clean of mud the tired limbs of the hungry beasts; preparing their rations of fodder, bedding them down with all the scrupulous diligence of an old-fashioned farm-labourer who has never been known to stint his duties, and who would finish his allotted task irrespective of the promptings of a master's eye.

As I think of him now particular scenes come before my mind. I remember meeting him one June night returning from the hayfields with his little daughter Nelly, a toadstool fairy, grave and responsible, perched upon the back of one of his enormous cart-horses. It was a midsummer evening when the atmosphere was aromatic with honeysuckle and clover, and as the obedient animal, with a jangling of harness and a shuffling of its hairy iron-shod feet, came to a standstill there was presented in the dusk one of those moments in a farm-labourer's life that seem to redeem the sweat and toil of his long working hours.

Montaigne used to say that when a man is faced with death all pretence must go and there is nothing for it but "to speak French." When from the nature of his disorder I knew that Herbert Parker would not live long I made inquiries as to his deportment. A week before the cruel cancer killed him our old Chaldon shepherd walked over the fields to see him and brought back to the village the news that although unable to speak above a whisper he was "happy." Evidently the wise earth known by him to her heart's root, had bestowed upon him at the last one of her most valuable gifts, the gift of endurance. "Men must endure their going hence, even as their coming hither: Ripeness is all."

JORDAN HILL

THERE is always a danger for people who are attached to a particular locality of showing unreason in the matter of change. Human beings are naturally conservative and existing conditions are never altered without offence. Perhaps the knowledge that our sojourn upon earth is in its very nature fugitive renders us all the more obstinate in resisting when it is in our power to do so this random principle which is the underlying law of the Universe. It is as though we hoped by preserving the appearance of a relative stability to stay the fearful torrent that will so soon sweep each one of us into the grave and in no time at all relegate our whole generation to oblivion.

The development for building purposes of the hill above the old Weymouth Coastguard Station affords in my own case just such an occasion for captious resentment. I discipline myself to remember that wherever human beings live poetry exists—I remind myself continually of the social gain to be derived from the activities of speculators in real estate. I try my utmost to take pleasure in the standardised gardens of the spick villas, and yet my spirit continues wilfully to regret the calm of this green hill before its exploitation. I think I would have been more reconciled were it not in serious jeopardy of having its very name changed. It would be a thousand pities if Bowleaze eventually became the official address of this modern suburb whose foundations are set upon ground out of which both Romans and Britons have in their time dug pot clay. Our fathers gave the hill the name of Jordan, just as they called the sedged trout stream which falls so pleasantly from the sailor-boy village of Preston down to the sea, Jordan River.

I once exasperated a companion at the Louvre by expending all my energy in a search for the picture Constable painted from the mouth of Jordan River. When it was found I observed with no small interest that the same rocks are still to be seen on the Redcliff Bay side of the brook, their shapes unchanged since the afternoon when Constable began his celebrated canvas. Have we in this change of names I am discussing, a saucy example of trade diplomacy? Bowleaze was originally the name of a narrow parcel of ground that lay about the mouth of Jordan River where an old stone bridge used to be and was never used to denote even the small cove, still less the ancient hill above. As the harmless appellation of an obscure scrap of Dorset ground it served a useful purpose, but lifted as it has been out of its original obscurity it is a vulgar and irritating innovation to the eyes of many of the older inhabitants of the Weymouth district. It was an ill chance that there should have been at hand a word so suitable for the purpose of modern advertisement—a word that so explicitly evokes the modern notion of leisure wherein mechanical transportation, short drinks, and the wireless take the place of country walks, reading, and a simple attitude of piety towards every manifestation of life. More than ever in these days if the spirit is to live it is necessary to illumine the commonplace with an awakened imagination, and to effect so charmed a mood the mind must be able to draw refreshment through direct contact with Nature and from meditations upon our mysterious and legendary past.

There used to be a ruined cottage on the top of Jordan Hill and during the year immediately following the Great War I was allowed, through the courtesy of Mr. Angus Scutt, to sleep in its overgrown garden. There was a deep well in this deserted walled-in plot with an ash-tree growing by it, an ash-tree as bowed by gales from the south-west as a Sherborne almshouse woman in her red cloak is bowed by age. In the spring-time ewes fed and lambs frolicked upon the sloping banks, and above every bank, thick-grown with nursery daisies, the stone-chats brabbled. Occasionally a shepherd living in a cottage behind my old friend Mr. Prideaux's dwelling-place would stop to have a word with me, resting his silver crook against the large uneven stones that ridged the wall's top. He would, with the dignified ease of a countryman, tell me the news of Dorchester market, or, looking over his shoulder across

Lodmoor, forecast the weather. I remember he differentiated between the kinds of nights he experienced in the lambing season: "proper dark nights," "moonshine nights," and "starshine nights."

It was the philosopher Heraclitus who first explained that all things in earth and heaven are subject to an ordinance of an irreversible flux. It appears, however, that through the agency of letters thought has attained to a semblance of permanence. In the *Iliad* there are three different kinds of trees mentioned as flourishing upon the plains of Troy—the oak-tree, the wild fig-tree, and the tamarisk. The schoolboys of Weymouth, whose good fortune it is to live in this sunny seaside settlement, must be as familiar with the tamarisk as was Hector's little son, recognising quickly its feathery glaucous foliage, so easily sensitive to the slightest stir of wind moving landwards from where, after the manner of the river Skamandros, the fresh water of the Jordan Brook mingles with the salt sea at the foot of Jordan Hill.

THE SEA! THE SEA! THE SEA!

TO children who have been brought up in an inland village anything in any way connected with the sea is full of a poignant romance. I am told that it is a common sight now to see seagulls upon the ploughed lands about Yeovil. This was not so when we lived at Montacute. It was the rarest thing then for these birds to fly over the garden and the appearance of one of them uttering its crying, so completely different from the sound of all other wild fowl, would never fail to cause us excitement. It has been suggested that the seagull inherits its singular voice, at once outlandish and articulate, from the pterodactyls, or early-flying reptiles, prodigious featherless creatures, which would go croaking across the newly-created earth.

In the large rambling Vicarage garden of our childhood no tang of salt was ever to be detected in the small rains that fell so continually upon those rich Somersetshire orchard lands, and even the south-west winds from the Atlantic had lost the rush and shriek of an authentic deep-sea gale by the time they had reached the tree-tops of Hedgecock, or vexed aged branches of the acacia, or beaten at last against the nursery window panes. In the spring of the year this inland quality of the garden was especially noticeable. Shells and seaweed, and mackerel with olive-green backs and rainbow-shining flanks—what had they to do with the sweet-smelling snow-on-the-mountain, with the large garden anemones, red and white, opening wide in the terrace walk, or with the summer sound of the lawn-mower at work for the first time in the yellow morning sunshine?

In those days my attention was always so passionately occupied with its childish interests that I seldom consciously took pleasure in the passing of the seasons, and yet it appears to me now that never since those mornings have I tasted the golden wine of April in so pure an essence, with my father on the drive before his usual time, his sermon finished out of hand at the sight of the first swallow flashing past his study window;

with the daisies and daffodil petals shining bright; and two eggs already in the hedge-sparrow's nest by the front gate, and the fugitive hours belonging, so it seems in the magical mirror of retrospective memory, not only to the importunate actuality of the moment, but to an antiquity lightly confederate with the eternal.

It was in the early hours of just such a morning that I set out with my brother Littleton to walk to the sea. I was fourteen or fifteen years old and to my young mind we seemed to be undertaking an almost impossible enterprise. My brother was ten years older than I in the very pride of his youthful manhood. We started very early fortifying ourselves with cups of coffee that had been kept warm in the kitchen oven overnight; and with our pockets full of provisions began walking southward. We went by Abbey farm over Batemoor past the outlying hamlet of Bagnel through the village of Haselbury Plucknett to Beaminster tunnel. We then made our way direct to the top of Lewesdon Hill where we refreshed ourselves with meat and drink. There under a fir-tree, and sheltered by gorse, we spent moments of intense happiness. More than half our walk was behind us, and before us, clearly visible, the wide blue sea sparkling in the sun. John Keats once said that he could not sleep all night so haunted was his imagination by Edgar's words in *King Lear*—"Can you not hear the sea?" To many the first sight of the sea is even more stirring than the sound of it. I have felt all my life a tremulous thrill, beyond all reasonable justification, when coming through Upwey tunnel on the way to Weymouth, the free waves under the White Nose cliffs first appear in a miniature seascape setting, across the rushy dykes of Lodmoor. Lewesdon Hill is not so tall a hill as its neighbour, Pilsdon Pen, with its triple oval-shaped fosse and vallum, but it reaches an elevation of eight hundred and ninety-four and commands a magnificent view of the coastline between Lyme Regis and Bridport, with Golden Cap proudly holding up his yellow sconce of oolite-sand against the azure of sea and sky.

This old West Country saying testifies to the striking dissimilitude between the two hills:

"*As much akin*
As Lewson Hill to Pilsdon Pen."

From Ham Hill, for example, their difference in contour is most remarkable, Lewesdon Hill of narrow compass rising sharply and with trees on its summit—Pilsdon Pen longer in shape and bare as a toad's back! It was the fishermen of the West Bay who gave them the names of the Cow and the Calf, which proves, I think that even viewed from the sea, though they may appear of the same kind, yet they must differ widely in size.

It is on the north-west slopes of Lewesdon Hill that Racedown Lodge stands, the house where Wordsworth stayed with his sister Dorothy as a young man, and where Coleridge came during the lovely haymaking weather of the June of 1797 to visit the author of *An Evening Walk*, and where there began the deep friendship between the two poets which was to have so momentous an influence upon English literature.

But neither of us then knew anything about Racedown Lodge, and if we had known about its proximity and the events that had taken place there just a hundred years before, I doubt very much whether our imaginations could have been diverted from the glad enchantments of our walk, with the English Channel stretched out before us and only a few miles of rich pastoral country separating us from it under the clear air of a cloudless spring day.

We left Broadwindsor to the east, with its Jacobean pulpit from which Thomas Fuller used to preach, and eventually reached the sea at a little hamlet called Seatown, situated a few miles eastward of Golden Cap and westward of Bridport Harbour.

I have never been there since, but in my memory a glamour still hangs over the place with its grassy lawns of freshest green resonant with the voices of children at play in the afternoon's long hours. With what delight we two ran across the shingle and sand to the edge of the salt water, actually arrived at the sea at last after walking down so many stitchwort lanes and over so many cowslip meadows! There to the east were the sheer cliffs

Came churchyard: William Barnes' grave, marked by the Celtic cross.

East Chaldon village.

The Sailor's Return at East Chaldon.

Remains of the gypsy track along the Dorset clifftop.

beyond West Bay that mark the very end of the Chesil Beach, that marks where the huge pebbles that are found at Portland, wide and flat as mill stones, have grown so fine as scarce to serve the turn of two fairies at pains to grind bride-cake-flour out of the seeds of vernal grasses.

This April walk from Montacute to the sea I have always thought of as marking one of the happiest days of my life, and it was this same walk that taught me to appreciate a particular verse in a strange and beautiful poem first read by me when I was in Africa:

> "And we remember
> How long ago the rain-wet celandines
> Pierced us with memories,
> With memories of things deeper than sleep or death
> And older than all the orbits of the planets.
> And we remember
> How from a long straight road—
> Somewhere—no matter where—
> While at our feet silver-weed and dandelion
> Laughed out of the hot dust,
> Somewhere—no matter where—
> We heard it; we knew it,
> The Sea! The Sea! The Sea!"

THE TOLPUDDLE MARTYRS

NOT far from my cottage on the downs is a barn known as the Old Barn. It is surrounded by a wall and there is a cow-pond within the enclosure. It is the very place for a man of philosophic temper to visit. It might have been built here on the bare hills for no other purpose than for human meditation. It resembles a diminutive Abbey Church standing within its garth. Its walls are constructed of huge blocks of chalk and if you enter the windowless building, crowded now with farm implements, and examine the masonry closely, it is soon revealed that the white flat surfaces have been used by generations of Dorset labourers as tablets for the simple graphetai of their days. Many of them have been content with recording on the walls of their "fretted vault" a date and the initials of their names; others commemorate their loves either in valentine fashion by two hearts arrow-pierced, or more often by the grossest phallic drawings such as evoked in ancient Egypt the symbol of the Ankh, the oldest of all human symbols. One of the dates is as early as 1725, so that many of these primitive inscriptions must have been cut by men whose arms had been made strong with the swinging of mediæval flails. The most common date scratched in is 1837, which marked Queen Victoria's accession to the throne; but 1830, the less happy year of the last labourer's revolt, also appears frequently.

Ever since the Enclosure Acts of the eighteenth century, the agricultural labourers of England have lost their independence. Their small-holdings were then taken from them, together with their arable and grazing rights on the common grounds, their fuel rights, and immemorial gleaning rights. Gone were their milk-white geese, their pigs and Cow Crumbock. In the autumn of 1830 the men of Chaldon Herring, who were then frequenting the Old Barn, joined with the Winfrith workmen in demanding a higher wage. The powerful squire of Moreton appeared before the village mob with one hundred and fifty special constables. The scene is described by a contemporary writer. "The men advanced rather respectfully and with their hats in their hands, to demand increases of wages." When after a parley they would not disperse they were charged by the posse of constables and three of their ring-leaders were taken away to be locked up in Dorchester Gaol.

It was this same Justice of the Peace, Squire Frampton, who with the help of Lord Digby, was responsible, after a covert hint from the Home Secretary, Lord Melbourne, for the persecution of the Tolpuddle Martyrs. It was the son of one of the gardeners of this same gentleman, James Frampton, who gave evidence against the six men, and it was Frampton who signed the warrant for their arrest and who committed them for trial.

William Ponsonby, a Member of Parliament for Dorset, was foreman of the jury, which consisted of farmers and dairymen —a linen-draper of Bere Regis being challenged because it was discovered that he was of the Methodist persuasion and had heard one of the Loveless brothers preach. The average rate of wage in neighbouring counties was at that time nine shillings and fourpence a week, and it was because of a plan to reduce the Dorset wages from seven shillings to six shillings that the men of Tolpuddle made their pathetic attempt to start a union. Without doubt their trial and conviction was carried through by class-interested magistrates under the connivance of the Whig Government.

Tolstoy declared that men at the Last Day would be judged by their hands and those whose hands had been made rough by manual labour would alone be allowed to enter into the Kingdom of Heaven. Certainly the labourers of England, who since the Enclosures have possessed less of the soil they cultivate than any other peasantry in Europe, have displayed the greatest fortitude in the endurance of their lot. With patient dignity they have trudged backwards and forwards to and from their work, their straw satchels over their shoulders. The Dorset grounds have been tilled for generations by peace-loving men who have never known holidays and whose toil, from the cradle to the coffin, has been taken as a matter of course. As lusty youths they have whistled and sung at the plough's tail, and as old men they have disturbed cutty-wren and chaffinch in the nettle-grown hedge banks with the cries of "Wok off" and "Com yer way."

This 17th of March is the hundredth anniversary of the opening of the Spring Assizes at Dorchester in the year 1834 . It is impossible to be unmoved by the glimpses we are given of these six labourers from Tolpuddle, of whom it was said "more honest men did not exist in the kingdom."

One of the papers supposed to be incriminating was discovered at the bottom of Betsy Loveless' work-box. The man Brines was witnessed against for having approached two labourers of Affpuddle, Lark and Legg, while they were at work thrashing, with a view to their becoming members of the Tolpuddle Grand Lodge. The Lovelesses and their four mates were thrown into a dungeon at Dorchester, and after having been sentenced to seven years' transportation were taken to Salisbury chained to a coach. The warder offered to remove the irons from the legs of George Loveless lest the people in the quiet cathedral city should stand and stare to see him pass. "I told him I did not wish for any such thing, as I was not ashamed to wear the chain, conscious of my innocence." The letters George Loveless wrote to his wife are full of an upright dignity. "I shall never forget the promise made at the altar: and though we may part awhile, I shall consider myself under the same obligations as though being in your immediate presence." They display also a meritorious lack of self-interest. "Be satisfied, my dear Betsy, on my account . . . I hope you will pay particular attention to the moral and spiritual interests of the children. Don't send me any money to distress yourself; I shall do well, for He who is the Lord of the winds and waves will be my support in life and death." When at the end of the trial the judge, Mr. Baron Williams, asked George Loveless if he had anything to say, he answered him in these memorable words: "My Lord, if we have violated any law it was not done intentionally. . . . We were united together to preserve ourselves, our wives and our children from utter degradation and starvation."

During the previous riots a young boy, Tom Brown, was charged with having written these rash words to Lord Sheffield: "Please, my Lord, I don't wish to hurt you. This is the case all the world over. If you don't get rid of your foreign steward and farmer and bailiff in a few days' time—less than a month—we will burn him up and you along with him. My writing is bad, but my firing is good, my Lord." This boy, seventeen years of age, had no lawyer to defend him, and when the Judge asked him if he would like to put any question, he replied simply: "That he hoped that his Lordship"—Lord Sheffield was present in the court—"would forgive him." The Judge answered "that his Lordship had not the power, and sentenced Brown to transportation for life."

As one reads accounts of the happenings of those days one longs for the powerful intervention of some honourable and magnanimous landed gentlemen of the kind that before now have not been unknown in Dorset. Where were the Lord Cranbornes, the Lord Shaftesburys, the Squire Sheridans, the Squires of Culver Dell, men diligent and strong to save their "humble and obedient labourers"?

A century has passed since those troubled months, and in the graveyards of Dorset the bones of the nobility, the bones of the gentry, and the bones of the poor lie side by side—the proud straight bones of leisure elbowed by the cheap bones of the labourer crooked with toil. To-day it is recognised that the values associated with pomp and pride, with property and power may easily become dangerous values to the Commonwealth. Wisdom tells us that the rarer and more sensitive rewards of life are not to be found in these flaunting and fugitive illusions.

I dreamed and in the Old Barn I saw a host of shadows come to listen once again to the words of the Book they had loved when they were still alive upon the broad flinty downlands. The shadows of ploughmen were there, together with the shadows of harvesters and rook boys, men with the clear-cut racial features commonly to be seen in Dorset lanes, heads as impressive as the heads of Bishops. Some were in smock-frocks, some in their shirt sleeves, and some with their trousers strapped about the knee. Silently they listened to the words of wrath and promise. "The Lord will roar from Zion . . . because they have sold the righteous for silver, and the poor for a pair of shoes . . . their treading is upon the poor and they take from him burdens of wheat."

With nitches of furzen on their shoulders and with drinking "owls" upon their elbow-crutches these spirit ancestors of the soil were congregated to hear the incantation of their wild herdsman prophet, telling how in a time and half a time their children's children would enjoy peace and plenty again in the pastures of the Frome and the Stour.

"When the ploughman shall overtake the reaper and the treader of grapes him that soweth the seed, and the mountains shall drop sweet wine . . . and I will plant them upon their land, and they shall no more be pulled up out of the land which I have given them, saith the Lord thy God."

AN OLD WEYMOUTH CURIOSITY SHOP

WEYMOUTH for its size and the number of its inhabitants is well provided with old curiosity shops. In these store-rooms of the past where treasured possessions of the dead are assembled together, it is possible to acquire memorable tokens of the times of our fathers. Within a stone's throw of the station walking southward is a very favourite shop of mine. The owner, Mr. Woodward, has a sensitive feeling for beautiful things, and is more concerned with spiritual values than with material gain.

To a man of understanding the bric-à-brac in these neglected depots of antiquity can in a poignant way bring to mind the pathos of human life. A shuttle-cock with each frayed feather still separately planted in the toy's leather cushion rimmed with red, can appear as a veritable symbol of life's swift flight. Where now are those comfortable Victorian interiors with their valances and antimacassars and well-established householders? Our religious ideas, our philosophic ideas alter with the passing of the generations. All things flow away, nothing remains the same.

It was in this quiet shop that I one day turned over the leaves of an early edition of *Pilgrim's Progress*, marvelling at the power of its prose, prose strong and idiomatic as talk in the open fields, and yet illumined by a passionate awareness of the mystery of earth-life. What poetic conceptions must have come crowding in upon the sturdy old Puritan as he sat on his bench in Bedford gaol making bootlace tags! From his "den," as he called it, he was able to see immortal shining rivers brim to their banks, and far away mountains from the upland slopes of which shepherds could discern, on clear evenings, the gleaming battlements of the City of God.

In the stubble-land behind White Nose I have often found a tiny flower shaped like a pansy. It is called heart's ease, and it is the very same flower that the shepherd lad was holding when in one of the rich meadows of the Valley of Humiliation, "as fruitful a place as ever the crow flies over," the Pilgrims heard him sing:

"He that is down, needs fear no fall;
He that is low, no pride:
He that is humble, ever shall
Have God to be his Guide."

Thomas Hearne tells us of a man who went half across England to see John Bunyan—and what a convincing picture we are given of the old man's simplicity: "When he came, he found John at home, and was received by him very civilly. He told him ye occasion of his coming, and said he had a great curiosity to see his study. 'There,' says John, pointing to a shelf, 'is all my study' which was nothing but a Bible and a Parcell of his own Books of ye *Pilgrim's Progress*."

It seems a long time since this celebrated allegory was published, and yet the cannon-ball lodged in the wall of the house near Weymouth Bridge belongs to an even earlier decade. I make no doubt that behind it the crevices are filled with Commonwealth dust, Restoration dust, Hanoverian dust, and with the dust of the time of the Napoleonic wars.

Such material objects provoke the mind to pass from one period to another, from one culture to another, and this is why so many reflective people are drawn to old curiosity shops.

Some years ago I was lucky enough to pick up in Weymouth a copy of Houdon's bust of Voltaire. I gave it to a sick friend, and he told me later how restoring to his spirits had been the extraordinary physiognomy of this octogenarian philosopher whose wit did so much to liberate the thought of Europe. Voltaire had sold his watches to Catherine the Great of Russia, had taught Frederick the Great to write poetry, and yet no political or Christian despotism was safe from the Satanic derision of this fashionable champion of the oppressed, whose faith in the power of tolerance and reason never faltered.

"The man who says, 'Believe as I do, or God will damn you,' will presently say, 'Believe as I do, or I shall assassinate you.'"

"Christianity must be divine since it has lasted 1,700 years despite the fact that it is so full of villainy and nonsense."

"The first priest was the first rogue who met the first fool."

"I do not agree with a word you say, but I will defend to the death your right to say it."

Until I was a young man there existed in Weymouth the most perfect of all curiosity shops. This ideal curiosity shop was situated somewhere in a side street leading from Chesterfield Terrace. Its small bay-window was crowded with objects that had to do with the sea—stuffed flying-fish, models of fully rigged four-masters, ditty-boxes covered with shells, and the flashing plumes of tropical birds. I used to imagine that the owner of this romantic shop was closely connected with far-travelling seafaring men, who would step across from the harbour taverns to deposit behind these small panes of glass treasures collected from the uttermost ends of the world.

It was from this shop that as a child I once bought a sea-horse, and I remember, as I carried it away past the place where in summer the goat-carriages stand, how it awakened my boy's mind to the wonder of life in its multiple infinitely varied manifestations. The ancients had a theory that every land creature had its double in the ocean. To look at a sea-horse is to believe this hearsay. Their heads resemble horses' heads in miniature, though, it is true, executed with one or two superfluous flourishes, such as one sees on the Knight in a collection of chessmen.

There was in this same shop a shell shaped like a trumpet, and on one occasion I was permitted to hold it to my ear. Its smooth ivory-like surface was as splashed and spotted as the leaf of a wood orchis, and very clear from the twisted orifice of this mottled conch there came to me the regular sound of small waves breaking over white sea-urchin sands under the palm-trees of an enchanted island. For some unaccountable reason this seashell music audible to me across so many intervening years is still associated in my mind with my lifelong confidence that a day will come when there will be a return of the golden age and men and women will once more be allowed to be happy.

HIGH CHALDON

THE village of Chaldon Herring is hidden away in the downs a little to the west of Winfrith. It possesses some ancient stones to remind its inhabitants of the fugitive centuries. The most important of these is the old font in the church. This is the work of Saxon masons. The second stone of consequence is the base of the mediæval cross which still stands on the village green. In *Foxe's Book of Martyrs* there may be read a Reformation rhyme that mentions a Chaldon Cross to which pilgrimages used to be made. I first took this allusion to refer to the cross on Chaldon Herring green, but on consulting with the late Mr. Charles Prideaux we discovered that there was another village of the same name, another Chaldon, or "Calfdown," somewhere in Kent, and that it was the tall crucifix of this other village that had inspired the rude verses.

The Chaldon Herring "holy stone" stands to the west of the village green opposite the post office, and suggests in shape a roughly hewn stoup, five times larger than the famous stoup to be seen in Broadmayne Church. This natural stoup at Chaldon is so large that it is easy to fancy it might once have been honoured in a cathedral porch, might once have held in its hollow a sufficiency of lustral water for the blessing of an urban population crowding over cobbled stones. The stone now remains in unassuming simplicity, bereft of clerical privileges, an accidental, unnoticed receptacle for the wild rain! On tremulous spring evenings when the village hedgerow banks are fresh mantled with parsley, with the broad shining leaves of lords-and-ladies, and with celandines fading to silver, an utter sense of dove-like peace will often gather about this uneven rustic lawn so happily consecrated by the ephemeral voices of children, as, with bright eyes and confederate mischief, they dance towards the lucky future.

The principal topographical feature of the village is High Chaldon. High Chaldon is a solitary hill, unconnected with any of the great downland ranges. Smoothly it heaves itself out of cowslip meadows to stand with broad back under the clouds. High Chaldon overlooks and dominates the village after the same manner that the Acropolis dominated Athens. My brother, Mr. Theodore Powys, has always appreciated the poetry of its presence, and he has allowed his powerful imagination to brood much upon it. It is at the foot of its north side that his Jar's stone may be seen, and the great isolated down is well known to all his readers as Madder Hill. There is gorse on the hill's crest and also a tall hedge.

In spite of the fact that High Chaldon stands two miles or more inland it always suggests proximity to the sea. This impression may partly be caused by the flocks of herring gulls that in wet weather come sailing in from the south to settle upon its green turf. At the hour before dawn after a rainy night they will be there in large numbers, as it were flocks of fairy-tale geese, white as snow, advancing on their webbed feet, this way and that, in search of their humble victuals. Here too, in the summer evenings, enormous cart-horses may be seen strengthening their huge limbs with a harmless diet of sweet grass; while through the chill weeks of January and February melancholy ewes, with restless Celtic eyes, have year after year anxiously mothered their young. On the hill's northern slope, a little above Jar's stone, there are badger sets. The catacombs of these friendly, berry-eating animals must penetrate deep into the heart of the hill. In old days I would always go to examine their footmarks imprinted in the mud under the nettles. Though dwarfed they reminded me of the spoors of the grizzly bear I used to come upon above the timber line in the Rocky Mountains.

Recently I stayed a month in lodgings in Brunswick Terrace at Weymouth. My cot was placed in a bow window of one of its charming old-fashioned houses, and I very naturally spent many hours examining the coastline where in the years of my strength I had often been so happy. I found that in clear weather it was possible to see a great deal with the naked eye. The Norman Chapel on St. Aldhelm's Head was visible, the grave of Caractacus was visible, the smuggler's boat on the top of White Nose was visible, the Merlin thorn was visible, and that outlandish natural monument of chalk in the undercliff below White Nose which for centuries has stared blankly towards Portland with forehead villainously low.

Presently, as I examined the rim of the down that meets the sky above Holworth House I observed a perceptible break in its clear outline. What I saw suggested that there was a furze-grown barrow somewhere in the fields above the old Commonwealth barton known as Sea Barn. I do not suppose there is an elder tree, thorn tree, holly tree, or gorse bush which is unknown to me in those fields, and it puzzled me to see a furze-grown tumulus where none to my knowledge had ever stood. I had by my side a pocket field-glass, and as soon as I had looked through it the mystery was solved. It was the topmost crest of High Chaldon that I was scanning, with the hill's grassy summit clearly discernible in front of its familiar windswept hedge. I was profoundly interested by my discovery. For more than forty-five years I have at various times narrowly examined the contours of the celebrated line of cliffs as they appear from Weymouth, but it had been necessary for me to reach the age of fifty before discovering that High Chaldon could be seen. It is possible that it may only be visible from the upper windows of the terraces and not from the Esplanade at all.

Many people not as familiar with the various landmarks as I am regarded my discovery with extreme scepticism. For some days I was at a loss as to how to convince them. Eventually I thought of this plan. I made arrangements that a flare should be lit at eight-thirty on a certain night on the top of High Chaldon. The selected evening happened to be a rainy one and I gave up all hope for the success of the plan. It seemed scarcely worth while even to look out of the window at the appointed time so dark was the night. Then suddenly the light appeared and I watched it burning for at least two minutes—a flame unaccountably suspended in the sky. Beyond all possible dispute my discovery was thus vindicated.

CERNE ABBAS

IT is strong testimony to the Englishman's good sense that the Cerne Giant on Trendle Hill has been allowed to remain unmutilated throughout the centuries. We can hardly doubt that it has been in serious jeopardy during several periods of our island history, but neither piety, purity, nor prudery has proved strong enough to overcome our English reverence for tradition, for everything that belongs to the past. The terrifying appearance of the Cerne Giant is emphasised by the smallness of his round onion-shaped head and by the hideous spider-like proportions of the crooked limbs, while to over-sensitive observers the figure's "brutish sting" symbolises the final triumph of appetite over intelligence. The chaste reticence of the monks must often have been outraged by the monster's figure as they looked up to it from the monastery. Many an honest Puritan must have eyed it askance from under his broad black hat; and during the decades of Queen Victoria's reign it must have offered an uncivil affront to the refined susceptibilities of the ladies and gentlemen, who in comfortable carriages smelling of expensive upholstery hot in the sun, rolled along the dusty roads from Sherborne to Dorchester. It is fortunately now out of danger, having been scheduled as a National Monument. It is strange to consider how this crude affirmation of life, deep dug in the chalk, overshadowed Aethelmar's Abbey from the day of its foundation in nine hundred and eighty-seven till the day of its fall in the sixteenth century, and indeed bids fair to outlast the dream of grace the cloistered retreat was built to establish.

If, however, stark carnality stands unrebuked upon the downs, below in the village of the beautiful valley it is possible for a man to recapture the very breath of Christianity in all the freshness of its innocence. It hovers above the blue water of St. Augustine's hallowed spring, evasive as the light from a triple rainbow when thunder clouds are in the sky; it envelops the ruined gatehouse waiting through long nights and days patient in its decay; it emanates through the subtle air from the lovely image of Mother and Son in the canopied niche on the tower of the parish church.

The last time I visited Cerne I was with Mr. Ernest Moule, a man of wide culture and of natural piety. It was under his instruction that I was initiated into this open secret of Dorset and was able for myself to feel the indefinable aura of religion still lingering about these shadowed fields, now visible, now invisible, like the pale flowers on summer blackberry brambles, indeterminate to dim corporeal sight and yet their presence so soothing in the gaudy days of early July. We passed a shepherd in one of the Cerne meads sitting under a hedge in the shade of a typical Dorset thorn-tree, a thorn-tree whose branches had all been bended to the north by continual wild winds from the West Bay. The sun was shining and the man on this "delectable mountain," with his dog and bright pastoral crook, was whittling away at a stout hedgerow stick as a support for one of his hurdles. It was impossible not to be reminded of the heart's wish of that ineffectual prince, one of the gentlest and most pathetic of English kings, who so yearned to pass his days in this very manner!

"O God! Methinks it were a happy life
To be no better than a homely swain;
To sit upon a hill, as I do now,
To carve out dials quaintly point by point. . . ."
". . . So minutes, hours, days, months and years,
Pass'd over to the end they were created,
Would bring white hairs into a quiet grave.
Ah, what a life were this! How sweet! How lovely!
Gives not the hawthorn bush a sweeter shade
To shepherds, looking on their silly sheep,
Than doth a rich embroider'd canopy
To kings that fear their subjects' treachery?"

And it was, so we presently remembered, this unlucky monarch's own queen, Margaret of Anjou, who had actually enjoyed the hospitality of the religious house here before the battle of Tewkesbury which ruined her cause. She had landed at Weymouth with a small French force on April 14th, 1471, only to learn of the defeat of her party under Warwick at Barnet, and it was beneath the sparrow-twittering roof of Cerne Abbey that she strengthened her spirit for her last desperate struggle; her young son, who was so soon to be pitifully murdered, still alive and breathing at her side! She arrived at the Abbey at that period of the year between the time when the monks were heartened by the sight of the first swallow over their stream and the time when the call of the cuckoo is first heard from Dorset elms already in tender leaf; at the time when the woodsmen of the Abbey were treading upon beds of garlic in the forest of Nether Cerne, and ladysmocks and kingcups were opening to the cockcrow sun in the home pastures. What was the nature of the thoughts that floated through the head of this proud French dame in her Dorset bower of piety, as, with no sanctified intention, she prepared once again to fight blindly for the royal rights of her darling child whom she had suckled with the dragon's milk of her own white paps and was so soon to see stabbed to death by perjured Clarence?

With the sure inspiration of genius it is Thomas Hardy who has preserved for us in literature the very spirit of this haunted Cerne district. His romantic poem, "The Lost Pyx," is charged with mediæval Christianity. The Cross-in-Hand is the subject of the poem, that strange monolith that even yet stands in solemn isolation on the top of the downs a little to the right of the road that runs westward from High Stoy.

According to Mr. Hardy this remarkable stone was planted here by an Abbot of Cerne to mark the spot where a miracle happened. This ecclesiastic in his younger days, as a hedge priest, had been wakened from sleep by a call to go to the deathbed of a labourer whose cottage was far away across the hills. The night happened to be one of those dark, wild, wet nights that frequently break over Dorset in the autumn, and the clerk pretended not to hear the voice of the messenger, but sluggard-like, turned again on his goose-feathered pillow. Then in a dream the voice of God called to him, and leaping out of his bed at so magisterial and awful a summons, he fled through the driving rain, only to discover upon his arriving at the cottage that his pyx, the metal box used for holding the wafer, was lost:

> "Then in dolorous dread he bent his head:
> 'No earthly prize or pelf
> Is the thing I've lost in tempest tossed
> But the Body of Christ Himself.'"

As best he could he retraced his way through the pitchy darkness, sometimes on hands and knees. Suddenly he noticed a light shining from heaven and when he reached the place he saw that the hallowed casket was surrounded by wild animals from the Dorset woods. A stag from Honeycomb knelt by it: a grey badger from the ferny hollow of Glanville Wootton, the thick knees of its legs of uneven length religiously flexed; a sensitive witch hare from a near-by turnip field also worshipped; and by her side Master Reynard, the red fox from the bottom of Green Lane, with the red squirrel from the tree-tops; the stoat that knows no fear from his fierce face to the end of his tail tufted with black hairs, knelt shoulder to shoulder with his plump slave, the clover-fed rabbit; and the obstinate, flat-headed, self-absorbed mole was there also in "pause profound," and a godless rat, and a shy, terrified field-mouse, with small, cold prying nose. From Melbury Bubb to High Stoy the rushing gale went shrieking by, but within the charmed circle of quaint prayer all was whist and still. These soulless unredeemed animals had gathered to adore and to preserve from harm this sacramental token of the heart-breaking mystery of life upon earth!

> "Then the priest bent likewise to the sod
> And thanked the Lord of Love,
> And blessed Mary, Mother of God,
> And all the saints above.
> And turning straight with his priceless freight
> He reached the dying one,
> Whose passing sprite had been stayed for the rite
> Without which bliss hath none."

The Durdle Door.

Weymouth: street scene.

A FAMOUS WRECK

IT is always interesting to trace a great man's association with the particular locality of our allegiance. We have in the letters of William and Dorothy Wordsworth delightful glimpses of the poet's stay in the old eighteenth century house of Racedown which stands under Lewesdon Hill, in Dorset. The house was lent to the poet rent free by John Frederick Pinney, though Mr. Pinney's father, a rich Bristol merchant, was left under the impression that Wordsworth was paying regularly for it. It was here that, quit of worldly worries, he was for the first time able to settle down to an existence of calm, uneventful days suitable to his temperament. He chopped logs for the firing, went to fetch provisions for the house, and once a week walked into Cruikhern (Crewkerne) for his letters.

The poet and his sister arrived at Racedown in the month of November, 1795. Ten years later another event occurred which was to connect in a particularly sad way the Wordsworth family with the county of Dorset. This was the tragic loss of the East India merchant vessel, the *Earl of Abergavenny*, one of the finest ships in the Company's service, on the Shambles, a reef of rocks lying a little to the east of Portland. Many lives were lost, amongst them being that of Captain John Wordsworth, the poet's younger brother, who was in command of the unlucky merchantman. The *Abergavenny*, during the morning of the disaster, had been beating about in the West Bay with her jibboom in, and the mizzen top-gallant mast lying on deck. At three in the afternoon a pilot was taken on board. As the vessel neared the Shambles, today guarded by a Trinity House lightship, the wind suddenly dropped. A strong westward drifting tide was running, and the *Abergavenny*, caught in "the Race," was carried on to the dreaded rocks. "Pilot, you have ruined me," exclaimed Captain John Wordsworth, as he realised what was about to happen. She struck the rocks at five o'clock, while it was still daylight, though the February evening was already beginning to close in.

In the vain hope that he would be able to shoot the *Abergavenny* over the reef, Captain Wordsworth ordered the topsails to be hoisted. The wind, however, had now shifted to the north-east and was blowing fresh off the downs from Culliford's Tree. For two hours the ship could not be budged. With three or four feet of water in her hold she kept swinging backwards and forwards, now to starboard, now to port, as the force of the tide or the force of the surf took possession of her. So violent were the shocks sustained by the ship that the officers and men were scarcely able to stand on the deck. In order not to alarm the passengers on board, valuable time was allowed to pass before orders were given for eighteen signals of distress to be fired.

At seven o'clock the *Abergavenny* freed herself, but she was now taking water so fast that Captain Wordsworth judged the best chance of saving her was to hoist all sail in the hope of being able to run her on to Weymouth sands, though how he proposed to do this in the teeth of a brisk wind is not clear. The carpenter presently, however, appeared upon deck announcing that he could do no more and that the ship must inevitably go to the bottom in a few minutes. This news was reported by the chief mate to the Captain. "It cannot be helped. God's will be done," answered John Wordsworth.

The *Abergavenny* foundered. Many of the men were washed overboard as she went down. Captain Wordsworth was observed for a few moment's swimming in the sea, but was soon lost to sight. Where she sank the bay was shallow enough to leave her masts above the surface of the water. A shocking scene immediately ensued. All who had not been washed overboard began clambering into the hurricane-torn shrouds, after the manner of rats making the utmost shift to escape death. One seaman, finding his leg held by a passenger and the progress of his climb to safety impeded, took out his clasp knife and cut off the offending fingers, so that the unfortunate wretch fell back into the sea. A woman passenger, in her terror, lacerated with her teeth the arm of her husband as he was trying to help her to a better position. Shouts and cries and shrieks of panic rose to the heavens, a volume of incoherent sound carried over the wind-scourged sea.

The freezing gale continued to blow across from Bincombe Down, adding to the horror of the scene, while huge waves every few moments broke against the flapping canvas. An unknown vessel passed close. She was "a sloop-rigged vessel with two boats astern." She disappeared into the night without offering any assistance. Continually people fell from the rigging, overcome by the cold or the difficulties of their positions, to mingle with the bodies of those already drowned, which kept washing against the lower sails half submerged in the sea.

Small boats presently appeared and began navigating near the unhappy wreck, but out of a not very honourable caution, they did not venture too close lest they should be swamped by so many unnerved men and women desperate for life. Slowly the wild, dark hours went by. A few people preserved themselves by balancing on floating wreckage. One man, the ship's joiner, floundering in the waves, managed to reach a launch which had floated away with the live stock that were to have been used on the voyage—sheep and cows. He climbed into the rudderless raft and was saved along with the animals.

It was not until the small hours that two sloops appeared. These vessels, anchoring near-by, succeeded in taking off the remaining survivors in good order, twenty at a time; and conveyed them, safe and sound, into Weymouth Harbour. Captain Wordsworth's body was washed up on Weymouth beach some weeks later. De Quincey asserts that he was buried in the Isle of Wight, but he evidently mistook the word Wight for Wyke, for the unlucky sea captain, aged thirty-two, lies in the churchyard of the original mother church of Weymouth, together with many of his own passengers and seamen.

The *Abergavenny* came to rest with twenty-seven feet of water over her upper deck. She heeled over a little to one side. The hope was for a long time entertained that she could be "weighed." Much of the valuable cargo was eventually recovered by a man named Tomkins, with the aid of a forcing air-pump, but she herself is still below the surface.

I have been told that deep-sea anglers who favour the Shamble "grounds" often bring back to Weymouth with their catches of bright fish, encrusted souvenirs from the wreck. Generations of flickering whitebait have gone sharking through the gaping portholes on the look-out for their invisible victuals. Generations of conger eels have wound their way in and out of the jointed timbers. She is there summer after summer, when the beautiful curving bay is happy with visitors from distant Dorset villages, and when a poet can stand under the August sun entranced

And see the children sport upon the shore
And hear the mighty waters rolling ever more.

William Wordsworth had by this time married and had left Dorset to live, together with his sister Dorothy, at Dove Cottage, on the edge of Grasmere. Richard Wordsworth, the poet's elder brother, broke the ill-news in the following letter:

Staple Inn,
Feb. 7th, 1805.

MY DEAR BROTHER,

It is with the most painful concern that I inform you of the loss of the ship Abergavenny *off Weymouth last night. . . . I am told that a great number of Persons have perished, and that our Brother John is amongst that number. . . . The ship struck against a Rock, and went to the Bottom. You will impart this to Dorothy in the best manner you can, and remember me most affectly. to her, and your wife, believe me*

Yours most sincerely,
RD. WORDSWORTH.

This news completely overwhelmed the peaceful household for several weeks, and the letters written during the period are full of pathos:

We have done all that could be done to console each other by weeping together. I trust we shall with the blessing of God grow

calmer every day. I cannot say anything at present more favourable than that we are all free from bodily illness, and do our best to support ourselves. I was useful to Dorothy and Mary during the first 12 hours which were dreadful, at present I weep with them and attempt little more.

Matthew Arnold, in after years, comparing Wordsworth to Goethe, charged the English poet with "averting his ken from half of human fate," and true enough it was that Wordsworth had small experience of human misery and only knew of those natural sorrows which are sometimes named "visitations of God." The news of his brother's death shocked him out of his customary complacency and compelled him to reconsider ultimate questions. After so heartless a calamity, how was it possible to justify the ways of God to men? It could only be done through a belief in a future life!

"Why," he writes, "have we sympathies that make the best of us afraid of inflicting pain and sorrow, which yet we see dealt about so lavishly by the Supreme Governor? Why should our notions of right towards each other, and to all sentient beings within our influence, differ so widely from what appears to be His notion and rule, if everything were to end here? Would it not be blasphemy to say that, upon the supposition of the thinking principle being destroyed by death, however inferior we may be to the great Cause and Ruler of things, we have *more of love* in our nature than He has? The thought is monstrous; and yet how to get rid of it, except upon the supposition of another and a *better world* I do not see."

In the same letter he gives us a glimpse of his brother's last moments as they had been described by one of the survivors:

A few minutes before the ship went down, my brother was seen talking with the first mate, with apparent cheerfulness; and he was standing on the hen-coop, which is the point from which he could overlook the whole ship, the moment she went down, dying as he had lived, in the place and point where his duty stationed him.

A little later in the same letter he quoted these words from Aristotle:

It is the property of fortitude not to be easily terrified by the dread of things pertaining to death.

POXWELL STONE-CIRCLE

I WOULD venture to say that it is impossible to walk a hundred yards across any ploughed field on the Dorset Downs without coming upon worked flints. Our Dorset seacoast hills must have been great centres for traffic in such primitive instruments. Often I have been astonished at the number of artifacts turned up by a plough in a single length of furrow. When, however, one recollects, that the new stone age, the Neolithic age, lasted certainly for fifteen to twenty thousand years there is not so much to wonder at, flint being a substance imperishable, remaining unaltered in shape for millennium after millennium.

It is a strange sensation to see lying on the rough tilth a finished implement in all its perfection, its original polish still preserved. The imagination strains to recreate an exact picture of those far-off days when the beautiful object was last consciously handled by human fingers, last consciously apprehended by a human mind! Shepherds and ploughmen in mediæval times did not fail to notice that some of the stones they picked up had been artificially improved; and forthwith, attributing the marks of careful chipping to the craft of fairies, they gave the name of "elf-shot" to all worked flints. And in truth many of the treasures we find on the downs were manufactured on so small a scale that they never could have been of any practical use, designed, as it would seem, either to serve as playthings for children, or for the fulfilment of some ceremonial purpose. I have found many such "pigmy" flints, as well as two perfectly modelled but infinitesimal arrow-heads, that surely could not have been used for killing game larger than a shrew mouse or a wren. Of course the weapons and instruments of every-day use are far more common and I have picked up many hand-axes, many hammers, adzes, hoes, pocket-knives, saws; and what are known as "scrapers," that is to say, oyster-shell shaped flints used for ridding the inside of deer skins still "green" of adhering flesh and fat. It is no easy matter to envisage these long periods of time between the last Ice Age and the first Celtic invasions when generations of shy Iberians and of still more primitive tribes experienced the gift of life. We ourselves have little enough capacity for reflection and speculation, but the naïve acceptance of life's phenomena of these men was even more infantile than is ours. It would seem, as those interminable periods went by and the employments of hunting and berry-gathering were abandoned for the more stable occupations of domesticating animals, that human reliance on magic steadily gave place to forms of religious confidence.

From Egypt rumours spread far and wide and the most learned antiquarians to-day do not hesitate to assert that Avebury and Stonehenge owe the form of their structure to influences that were first conspicuous on steaming flats of the Nile. In Dorset there are still existing many lesser examples of the same elementary style, sanctuaries formed of monoliths patiently arranged under the impulse of religious feeling, so that in a particular place hallowed by custom, fertility rites could be practised, or men could bow the hairy scalp before the rising sun of the summer solstice.

Of all such sacred parcels of ground, to me the most attractive is the diminutive stone circle on the crest of the hill eastward from Poxwell. The tallest of the stones of this religious ring would not be as high as the golden fleece on the back of a Dorset Horn ram. Yet every one of the stones of the ring's inner circle remains in place. If a wayfarer walking from the Weymouth direction after passing Upton Lane goes through the first field gate beyond the keeper's cottage he will come upon the circle on the hill-top some hundred yards above the quarry. It is a Stonehenge in miniature, though in actual fact no bigger than a fairies' orb.

There are occasions when it would seem that these lowly stones, unnoticed by many, gather to themselves an elemental force. Thirty centuries have gone by since they were first "planted" by the muscular hands of rank skin-clad men. To experience their influence it is best to come here alone and at midnight. At such an hour each tree in the ancient Trenchard wood below stands clear under the stars, and it is as though the patient timber with its trembling leaves gave strength and understanding to the mind. To kneel here when the homeless wind rustles through the coarse tufts of grass unpulled by the moist mouths of the winter stock, is an action calculated to break the bondage of cowardly thought. These unostentatious stones are very ancient. The memory of stone is older than the memory of wood, though the memory of the vegetable world is very long. In California I was once shown redwood trees quick with sap whose span of life far outstretched the history of Christianity, living trees which on the afternoon of the Crucifixion had already achieved the vigorous growth of centuries.

If the desperate magnanimity of Jesus has failed to soften the lawless hearts of men—in what other fairy enchantment can we put our hope? As timber wolves the nations band together in packs thirsting for blood. The omens are heavy for a day of bitter destruction. Blind mouths are industrious to support tyrannic power for ends of aggression. For a good reason may we touch the earth with our foreheads in the stone circle at Poxwell, in the oldest of all places of worship in Dorset, bringing back to our minds before it is too late the warning words of the poet Hesiod. To the old Bœotian farmer, as to the prophets of the Old Testament, the real poignancy of the world's drama is to be looked for in the unending struggle between frowardness and reason. Vehemently did Hesiod's spirit reluct from the terrible visitation "when Envy, foul-mouthed, delighting in evil, with scowling face, will go along with wretched men one and all," and when the spirit of compassion and the spirit of justice, "with their sweet forms wrapped in white robes, will go from the wide-pathed earth and forsake mankind to join the company of the deathless Gods; and bitter sorrows will be left for mortal men, and there will be no help against evil."

ST. ALDHELM'S HEAD*

IF Golden Cap is the highest and White Nose the proudest of the Dorset Headlands, St. Aldhelm's Head may well be described as the most romantic. I remember when I was a boy looking out of my grandmother's house in Brunswick Terrace at the wonderful coastline to the east of Weymouth and being told by my father that the furthest of all the cliffs, faint as a summer cloud on the horizon, was St. Alban's Head. The promontory in those days was always called by this name, and is still so called by many people despite the fact that a chapel dedicated to Saint Ealdhelm has for seven hundred years stood on the forehead of the great cliff, a sure testimony to the verbal corruption that would substitute the name of the martyr saint for that of the first Bishop of Sherborne.

It is known that Saint Ealdhelm possessed an estate near Wareham and that it was on this land that he built a church on the occasion of his waiting for a ship to carry him out of Poole Harbour to Gaul on his way to Rome. This Saxon church in due time fell into ruin, and yet by a miracle for all the rushing gales that drive over the Island of Purbeck, a portion of its roof for centuries afforded a canopy broad enough to protect the altar stone from wind and weather and desecrations by wild birds. In William of Malmesbury's day, at the beginning of the twelfth century, the masonry of this church was still to be seen and he recounts that even in its decayed condition the building had provided shelter for generations of Dorset shepherds, the men having learnt from experience that in the worst storms no drop of rain ever fell on the sacred slab.

It has been generally assumed that the site of this church was near Wareham, but I would direct the reader's attention to the

* When referring to the Headland I have followed the customary spelling Aldhelm. When referring more particularly to the Saint I have followed the spelling used by my old school master, Mr. W. B. Wildman, who explains that the name of the aristocratic Saxon Bishop originally signified "old helmet."

fact that there are not now, and never have been, shepherds on Wareham Heath. Folk of this kind are, however, as common as thistles on the downs near the sea. Here their figures are to be seen any hour like the forked letters of a black alphabet against the sky line, and, if, as I believe, the present chapel of St. Aldhelm's Head stands upon the very spot where the miraculous ruin once was, the reference to desecration by wild birds would be particularly apposite, for the present "mighty mass" is a favourite place for the sea gulls, to settle upon. The evidence as to the situation of the original church exists at the British Museum in William of Malmesbury's own handwriting, and runs as follows: "Locus est in Dorsetensi pago ii milibus a mari disparatus, juxta Werham, ubi et Corf Castellum pelago prominet."

The translation of this is:

"The place lies in the county of Dorset about two miles distant from the sea, not far from Wareham; where Corfe Castle also commands the main."

Although the words "two miles from the sea" go somewhat against our theory the reference to Corfe strengthens it, for the famous Castle Hill most certainly may be said to command "the pass" leading to the sea.

The story goes that Ealdhelm built the chapel so that he might have a suitable place in which to pray for good weather on his proposed voyage—and with such a preoccupation in his head what more favourable position could he have found than this high cliff-top, so much more appropriate to his purpose than any site in the vicinity of the low-lying estuary of Wareham? "Sweet it is, when on the great sea the winds are buffeting the waters, to gaze from the land on another's great struggles; not because it is pleasure or joy that anyone should be distressed; but because it is sweet to perceive from what misfortune you yourself are free." We have reason to believe that the Saint shared with the Psalmists and Prophets of the Old Testament the liveliest suspicion of the manners of the "great deep." In his essay in praise of Virginity he writes: "Virginity is dry land, chastity a harbour, married life the open sea."

The great Saxon ecclesiastic is fortunate indeed in the magnificence of the landmark that helps to perpetuate his name. What an impressive fragment of wild nature is presented by this Dorset cape! There is about the very approach to the headland a noble simplicity. As we pass from field to field we become more and more conscious that the tremendous stone foundations of the locality are only a little way below our shoe-leather. Yet this thin layer of surface soil upon which we tread is deep enough and fecund enough to grow acres upon acres of corn, the compact ears of which during the early days of August may be seen solid against the waves of the unharvested sea, gold upon blue! In this favoured month how wonderful to walk here! Every fleabane, every knapweed, every scabious and aromatic yarrow flower has in those properous days it own painted butterfly, and if you look back in your path in the late afternoon, you will be able to observe numberless insects crossing and recrossing the warmed atmospheric spaces in a myriad dancing flights.

In the spring-time it is different. The fields are bare then and few come this way. The Christmas shelters of the shepherds are still conspicuous in the lee of the long walls whose stones, every one of them, is hoar with crisp lichen. For these low walls with their bramble patches, elder trees, and signal thorns have protected the resolute bodies of hardy men through centuries of inclement weather. There is scarce a foot along any of these walls where shepherds have not couched with sacks over their shoulders and their thumbs greasy from the fells of the sheep they have been tending. They have waited patiently in these retreats, their honourable minds stubbornly obsessed with the case of this or that enduring ewe, which in a near-by solitary cote is labouring to bring a long-legged lamb, wrinkled and pathetic, into a world of sleet and the first Dorset daisies.

And what an occasion it is when the sea fowl begin to nest—cormorants, herring gulls, razor-bills, guillemots; and, above all, the puffins, sitting together like migratory parrots from the hanging forests of the Amazon, startling the sight with the tropical colouring of their broad chops!

It was just at this time of the year that I last visited St. Aldhelm's Head. The gulls were calling over the sea, the larks were in the air, the wheatears upon the grassy tussocks, and I was alone. While examining the sturdy rectangular chapel a foolish impulse persuaded me to press my head between the stones of the narrow lancet window, the only window that the building possesses. A trap to catch woodcock! Try as I might, I could not withdraw my head. Very nearly did I become pudding meat for those same sea-parrots I had so admired. When I did free myself it was at the cost of both my ears that were as sore as if they had been cropped in a pillory by a village beadle. A celebrated poem of St. Ealdhelm treats of eight principal vices that pester mankind. The most exacting examination at the Day of Judgement will never find me guilty of Acedia, the sin of taking no interest in life. If this adventure with the window is to be attributed to a supernatural correction I must have been shamed because I have so often been guilty of Kenodoxia, a word the Saint applied to the condition of spiritual intractability that is productive of heresies.

St. Ealdhelm was a kinsman of King Ina of Wessex, and there is something debonair and aristocratic about his attitude to literature. He was a great saint and a great gentleman, and, as the founder of Sherborne School, carried his scholarship with lightness and grace. This is well shown in his correspondence with Ealdfrith, the King of Northumbria, whom he taught to make Latin verses by composing a series of amusing riddles.

The ridge of the roof of the chapel on St. Aldhelm's Head is provided with a circular turret for a beacon-light, as is also St. Catherine's Chapel at Abbotsbury, both buildings having been used for centuries as primitive lighthouses. Is it my opinion that the existing chapel of St. Aldhelm's Head inherited this lighthouse tradition directly from the Saint's own church, whose fragmentary miraculously preserved roof may have served all through the Saxon period for such a purpose. After reading the following riddle, the answer of which is Lighthouse, it is hard to believe that St. Ealdhelm had not in his mind, as he composed the verses, the great headland that faced the sea, perhaps upon his own property, or, in any case, within easy riding distance of it:

> "High on the cliffs that front the thunderous seas,
> While the salt surf goes whistling down the breeze,
> Upreared was I, a solid and mighty mass,
> To show the sea-ways to the ships that pass.
> I never ploughed with sinuous share the main,
> And yet by signals from my lofty ledge
> I guide the wave-tossed wanderers to the shore;
> While murky clouds block out the stars of night,
> Flaming afar I stand a tower of light."

STALBRIDGE RECTORY

I REMEMBER once at Montacute asking my father many questions about his boyhood at Stalbridge. From my earliest childhood every scrap of information about my grandfather or about my father's life at Stalbridge had been cherished by me. The mere mention of the name of the stately old Dorset market-town had the power of stirring my imagination. My grandfather, who was born in the eighteenth century, only six years after the death of Dr. Johnson, held the living of Stalbridge from 1837 to 1867, and was buried in the churchyard there at the age of eighty, the same age reached by my father who died in 1923.

With the burial of my father in the Montacute Churchyard it seemed that the family memories of Stalbridge must be for ever at an end. This has proved far from the truth. Recently I happened to meet a native of Stalbridge, Mr. Henry Habershon, whose passion for the village and all that is connected with it, amounts to an obsession. I have never known anyone with such an infatuation for the place of his birth, anyone who husbands with such tenacity, with such depth of emotion, his long, long memories. The trees, the very stones of Stalbridge are sacred to him. As my grandfather was the Rector of his natal village for the first quarter of Mr. Habershon's life the Powys family is closely associated with his youthful illusions. Here therefore against all chance I had discovered someone who preserved in his melancholy head an inexhaustible store of ancient remembrances, capable of being transmitted to me as clear as if they had happened yesterday. He described to me my grandfather's carriage, recollecting even the precise livery of his postilion, so that I was able to see as plain as in old print the coach starting away from the Rectory gate for my grandmother to take the air through Marnhull, "passing by little Charley's favourite oak-tree," or for her to pay a call on Mrs. Yeatman at Stock House. From an absolute oblivion he could snatch back the very name of my grandfather's dog, and tell me how when he barked the echo could be heard by those walking in the street. He told of meeting my father and my Uncle Littleton one winter on the Sherborne Road "beating the snow off the high hedges with their sticks," and this casual reference, dropped without premeditation, seemed to give me a glimpse of my father's boyhood as though I myself had witnessed the incident with my own eyes, so convincing in its naturalness, and yet so difficult to connect with the dignity of my father's later years. He told of how my uncle challenged "the worst poacher in Stalbridge" to a boxing match behind the tall wall of the Rectory garden, and how the men were astonished at the number of rounds and the amount of punishment that my uncle, a mere youth, had taken, and how when in the end he was "knocked out," Mr. Habershon, who was bringing water from a near-by cattle trough, heard him say: "Don't let the old man know." In a letter to me this survivor from early Victorian times records the first occasion that he ever saw my father and uncle, and for me, a man of fifty, this recollection seems to penetrate into a past age beyond calculation.

"The first time I can remember seeing the two young gentlemen was when I was a small lad going past the old Cross I looked up Gold Street and I saw a large donkey with panniers on its back and one young gentleman in each and a man in charge, Sam Shepherd, who was living then in one of the Powys cottages on the top of Gold Street known as the Knap in those days."

I came upon a reference to this very donkey—under what exact parcel of Stalbridge turf are its long bones even now turning to dust?—in one of my grandmother's note-books, describing how my uncle when he was still unable to speak, would pull at his own baby ears so as to emphasise to my grandmother his satisfaction in the exaggerated length of those of the tall beast. She tells too with pride how my uncle before he was twelve months old would recognise my grandfather's step coming down the fine old staircase of Stalbridge Rectory, and would cry out: "Papa! Papa!"

Among some old family letters I came upon one from Dr.

Harper, the celebrated head master of Sherborne, the moral tone which, so much in advance of his age, matches some of Dr. Arnold's communications.

King's School,
Sherborne.
May 10*th*.

My dear Sir,

I am always at home of sheer necessity, and it is part and parcel of my daily work to talk over such matters as those now concerning your boy. I am very sorry that he has chosen the army. I am always sorry for every boy who does so, not only because it is no profession in reality but also because of the temptations into which he is so thrust. However in many points your lad is fit for a soldier and will be a straightforward brave fellow under any circumstances. . . . I am, dear Sir, Yours Sincerely, H. D. HARPER.

It interests me to remember that while my grandfather was at Stalbridge, Lord Sidney Godolphin Osborne, whose character I so much admire, was the Rector of Durweston further down the Stour. There could scarcely have been two men more different. In spite of his academic honours, for he won "a first" in both the classical and the mathematical tripos at Cambridge, my grandfather had an extremely simple nature, and I do not suppose ever had the slightest misgivings on the score of the social injustices of his period. Along with most of his contemporaries he seems to have taken the existing order of things as inevitable. He was, however, of a generous nature and gave a great deal of money away, never, so one old village woman told me, stepping out of the Rectory gate without a purse full of half-crowns to meet any unexpected call upon his charity.

While on a visit to London he met some of his Cambridge friends on their way to present a University address to the young Queen. He hired appropriate robes and went with them to the palace.

"We went to Buckingham House about two o'clock and were in due time ushered into the Throne Room, where sat Victoria having at the left hand Prince Albert with divers other notables. I was fortunate enough to get a good place and saw the Queen and Prince well. The Prince is good looking much like an English gentleman, as for her Majesty, I cannot say that her personal appearance is very engaging or imposing, but Pipsey will utter one of her indignant *grunts*, if I speak with less admiration than she deems fitting. The Duchess of Sunderland sat apart, retired, and looked a Queen, "aye, every inch a Queen."

The Ministers of State were present and on the whole it was very well to have for once been present at such a Spectacle. The Yeomen of the Guard and Beefeaters in the ancient costume were arranged in a picturesque manner in the Halls and on the staircases. The rush of the carriages was most awful, and the pressure through the gateways quite dangerous, reminding me forcibly of the contending crowds in my Proctorial Days at Cambridge.

I suppose I shall stay to Friday and shall hope to find my way back to the good old Rectory by dinner time.

I am your most attached and affectionate

L. C. Powys.

On the occasion of my father taking his honours degree, he wrote:

My dear Charley,

As the intoxication of success has now subsided a little, you can perhaps bear with the humble congratulations of the Old Folks. We are both very thankful to see you in so respectable a place in the Honours and we doubt not that this will be the beginning of a happy and prosperous career. . . . Littleton crosses to Ireland this evening from Plymouth. He takes with him the brown mare, by way of shewing her a little of the world. . . . I hope your purse held out against the University fees. I shall soon expect a letter from Mr. Perowne—

Ever your affectionate father,

L. C. Powys.

But there are more intimate scripts that used to be preserved in the tall study desk at which it was my father's custom to stand when he composed his sermons, and these writings show clearly that my grandfather possessed a deeply religious mind. All through his long life he never for one single moment doubted that he was under the care of an attentive deity. As a young man he had a bad fall from his horse at his home at Achurch in Northamptonshire and he puts on record his gratitude for his escape. Again as a man of forty, when he was a Fellow of Corpus, he had a serious misadventure. Sitting in his spacious rooms in the Old Court of the College—rooms which in my time were used by the present Bishop of Derby—he makes this entry:

"Another providential interposition. Much bruised by the wheel of my gig crushing me against the wall but thro' Mercy not materially injured. While I live will I praise the Lord. May I have grace to use the life which Thou so frequently preserves to My Glory in Christ Jesus."

Lastly at Stalbridge in the cold winter of 1864 he mentions falling outside the house of a certain Mr. Lewis, and inscribes these words at the end of the old service book that he used all through his life:

Jan. 20. "Thrown down heavily on Pavement and stone step at Mr. Lewis but providentially preserved from serious injury; all thanks and praise to Him who watches over His servant both in body and soul. He keepeth all our Bones so that Not one of them is broken."

To my mind, however, the most interesting of my grandfather's papers is a small parchment on which in the year after the Battle of Waterloo, at the age of twenty-six, he makes a formal dedication of himself to the service of God. "So that I may become a blessing to my generation," is one of the simple phrases he uses. As a schoolboy at Winchester he had spent "idle and unprofitable days," and steadfastly resolves to live for God's glory rather than "for my own selfish ease and gratification."

This document, sealed with the Powys crest, seems to have represented in his mind a kind of testamentary declaration of the spiritual purpose which was moving him at that period in his career; and which, in truth, was to direct his life for more than fifty years still to come. To me the devout words on this faded paper, already one hundred and eighteen years old, seem infinitely affecting. It is as though I were permitted to look at, to handle even, the scroll that had served as my grandfather's passport across the Delectable Mountains to the very gates of the Celestial City!

In these days, when the hazard of life becomes every year more apparent, how restorative to take sanctuary in the sound pastures of such a village as was Stalbridge in Queen Victoria's reign, when, under the persuasive influence of age-long human usage, every cranny of life was well caulked with the honest clay of wont and habit and bright polished with the shining resin of an unquestioning Faith. Those long slow years knew no treachery. Clearly I can see them pass into eternity. I can see my aunt Philippa, my father's half-sister, the Pipsey of my grandfather's letter, at the age of eight holding in her nursery at Christmas time a reception for the "poor old women of the village," like a silver-slippered princess enjoying the pleasing sensation of presenting each one of them with a new shilling out of her savings. I can hear the footsteps of my grandfather punctually every autumn evening going up the broad staircase, flat silver candlestick in hand. I can hear my father's very voice calling to his brother from those old rooms, and can see him in the pantaloon trousers of the day bringing in the first primrose for my grandmother, a service of grace which in after years he never failed to do for my mother. I can see him running along through the hay-seed meadows of midsummer to inspect his eel lines laid by the bank of some dark pool of the Stour, careful not to disturb the corncrake on her nest. Where was there opportunity for treason in such a life—son following father, son following father, in long generations of easy circumstance, with the confidence of an endless sequence of happy reunions beyond the grave? What perfidy could there be in the agglomerate atomies that made up the yellow and black stripes of the September wasp's abdomen as it hovered with drowsy murmur over the last King William pear at the bottom of the silver fruit basket? It was my grandfather's habit in winter and summer to dine at three in the afternoon, a custom he had retained from his bachelor days at Cambridge.

There were no misgivings, no uneasiness of conscience about society as it had been ordered under Providence. Year after year my grandmother continued to fill her precious albums with spatterings of seaweed, with delicate paintings of spring flowers, of sea-shells; never, however, forgetting to see that Maria, the cook, put the tea-leaves that had been used in the beautiful drawing-room teapot out upon the wooden settle beyond "Dash's kennel, so that poor people, by merely opening the back gate, could fetch them away."

In his old age at Weymouth when his mind was beginning to fail my father one day mysteriously disappeared from his house. My sister remembered afterwards that he had said good-bye to her with unusual formality before setting out for his morning walk. Actually he had gone to the Weymouth station, and procuring a ticket to Templecombe, had walked from there to Stalbridge presenting himself for tea in his old home where he was entertained with courtesy by his host. He settled himself in the parlour looking about him with a benevolent expression but spoke no word. In the late evening, thanks to the efforts of the station officials, news was telegraphed that an aged clergyman had been sitting for several hours on the Templecombe platform. He seemed to be in no trouble, his mind quiet and at peace, a happy old man who knew he was lost, but who was content to wait in benign confidence for the moment when he would again be looked after, again be found—perhaps by his daughter, perhaps by his wife, perhaps by his mother. I have often speculated as to the exact nature of the impulse that prompted my father to undertake so unexpected an adventure. Did he simply wish to revive in his mind old memories of his childhood, to remind himself for the last time through the sense of sight, before he entered the realm of dust and darkness, of the exact look of the mulberry-tree, of the chestnut-tree whose every bough he knew from climbing them as a boy? Did he wish to see again where his baby garden had been at the end of the nut walk, with its well-watered mignonette and large grave-faced pansies purple and yellow? Or as he approached near and nearer into his power, had Death, like an enchanter, cast a glamour over my father's faltering imagination so that he really came to believe that he had only to go back to the house where he was born to be welcomed once more by his brother, by his mother, and by his father, past all expectation clothed again in the sweet flesh of life, united and happy in those dreaming rooms of the ancient Rectory of Stalbridge in Dorset?

DEATH BY VIOLENCE

ALWAYS excepting the dawn, the most impressive hour of the day on the Dorset downs is the last twilight hour of a June evening. Along the horizons float the huge summer clouds, veils of a temple against the background of which are enacted the experiences of our transitory human lives, with their anxieties incident to husbandry, their shocks from the betrayals of death, and their deep rewards of love.

This twilight hour is rendered especially solemn by the herring gulls which are then breasting their way over the undisturbed valleys in absolute silence back to the sea. During the hour before the dawn these birds are full of clamour, making the sky above the flinty downs ring and ring again with their unregenerate calls. It has been suggested that the voices of gulls constitute the most primitive of all bird articulations, being inherited perhaps from the heartless screams that once whistled through the jagged beaks of the pterodactyls as they winged their flapping membrane sails against the flamingo-red sunsets of the Jurassic Age. It is possible that for this very reason the noiseless late evening flying of the sea-returning herring gulls is the more awe-inspiring.

A traveller watching these birds on their nesting ledges in the breeding season might well conclude that they were of as mild a temper as doves, so tender are they of their three nestlings, drab chicks round and fluffy as play-balls of wool, and yet at their peril hatched to life on a precarious precipice between two dizzy expanses of celestial blue! Such a judgement would be a mistaken one, for there exists no fowl of the air more ready to take advantage of the weak or wounded, pecking out living eyes or rending apart living flesh with rapacious avidity. Though not as truculent as the notorious black-backed gull, that merciless marauder of our sea-coast beaches, I have often observed them go out of their way to make an unprovoked attack on a passing raven should one of these venerable self-engrossed birds happen to cross their path.

Ravens are not naturally quarrelsome if left alone, but it would seem that their dark figures arouse the most vindictive emotions in other birds. The war between the ravens and the peregrine falcons, for example, is as never-ending as the war between the pigmies and the cranes, and I have seen one of these birds of Woden lose sable feathers when the hawk has been lucky enough to get in a stroke before the raven had had time to turn a somersault in mid-air, a feat it performs with surprising agility in order to be able in the critical moment of the "stoop" to confront the falcon with claw and beak. Should the peregrine press such an advantage too vigorously, the enormous bird with a few protesting croaks will drop slowly to the ground, where, standing four square amid the milk-wort and carline thistles, it knows that the boldest tercel will not venture to molest it further.

Yesterday three ravens were being attacked by a single herring gull far up over our valley. The gull should never have interfered with three birds at the same time. I watched the battle until they disappeared from my view. Five minutes later, however, the ravens returned over our cottage. I think they were a pair accompanied by a young bird not quite full grown. One of them was flying unusually low, and I noticed that it was performing the curious exercise of falling through the air with legs outstretched. It is possible that these erratic movements may have represented the bird's predatory exultation, for the herring gull was found later dead on the grassy track leading up the valley. It was brought to me and I examined it closely. An extremely neat puncture had been made in its cranium by the raven's heavy bill.

The herring gull's violent end in the full passion of life had preserved the resplendence of its savage hauteur unmarred. It lay on my counterpane undefeated. Its lower mandible was painted with a splash of orange-red as giddy as a sea-parrot's beak. Its back and wings were of softest grey, softer than the coat of a grey squirrel; and its breast feathers, thicker than those covering the wish-bone of a Michaelmas goose, were white as milk and as voluptuous to the touch as the abdomen of an eider duck. Its webbed feet were rough and of a dirty whitish colour, equally serviceable for propelling the bird along the surface of the waves as for sedately paddling it through rain-wet early morning grass alert for the lowly rustling of earthworms.

The pride of this sea bird's eye had not yet been dimmed. The white of the orb was watery and transparent as glass. The far-seeing pupils were bright and black. It was by means of these two tiny polished crystals of reflection that this incarnate spirit of the wind and the waves had received its impressions of the visible world—the flash of a mackerel's rainbow flank, the long-legged corpse of a new-born lamb abject under a gorse bush. It was by their aid that inaudibly each night it had been able to find its way back to the sea within the cloud horizons that enclose the life dramas of the men and beasts and birds sheltering on the chalk downs.

PORTLAND

I REMEMBER when I was thinking of returning to settle in England on the Dorset coast taking down from a bookshelf in an old house in Connecticut an encyclopædia containing a tattered map of Dorset with the Island of Portland stretching its bald bold turkey's head far out into the English Channel. In almost any map this peninsular must of necessity protrude as an emphatic appendage to the southern coast-line of England, conspicuous to the human eye, to the Chinaman's eye, to the negro's eye, to the Red Indian's eye, to the eye of a Church Missionary native idling over his lesson book under a palm-tree in the Cannibal Islands.

What a wealth of romance has surrounded this West Country promontory since the days of my earliest childhood! Its frowning forehead was familiar to me from Brunswick Terrace in Weymouth, towering above the magpie-speckled lighthouse on the "old" Breakwater. Rumours of it had reached my ears when I was a very infant. My father used often to appear with round flat pebbles for my mother and grandmother to paint pictures upon, and these, I was told, came from Portland; and when the weather had been particularly wild I would hear of my father and my elder brothers making an excursion to Portland to see the waves!

I cannot conceive of any portion of the English coast more calculated to arouse a boy's imagination than the Chiswell end of the Chesil Beach. It is possible even when the weather is rough to stand in comparative safety and look down into the dragon throat of the terrible bay. A prodigious Atlantic roller, visible for a long time to a rain-drenched onlooker above the turbulence of all lesser waves far out at sea, dashes itself at last against this huge natural breakwater, and a second later, its pride broken, withdraws with an irresistible suction down, down, down, foam and tumbling pebbles together, until with a snarl, the very ocean floor is, for the duration of a moment, exposed under the curved suspended arch of a tottering wall of water, high towering as a church steeple, broad and awe-inspiring as the Niagara in flood.

On a fair summer's morning how wonderful to stand on the famous sea-bank looking out over Dead Man's Bay, with wide-benched deep-water fishing-boats on every side, and the pebbles under foot spotted and blackened with fisherman's tar; the air smelling of green waves, of wind and sunshine; and with vast nets spread out everywhere to dry, loaded with cork floats five times larger in size than those that dangle on the puny spider-web Weymouth nets, brown nets with a mesh so stout that they could drag to shore an entangled mermaid for all her petulance. And the old stone tavern called the Cove Inn which stands on the top of the beach—was there ever such a hostel? The landlord once told me that during the worst winter gales the sea invariably reaches to its stone porch and goes pouring down on each side of the house to the sheltered village street below. What a view presents itself from its sarcophagus-like doorway in fine weather—the great sea beach with its wide-sweeping curve of twenty miles, the broad flecked acres of the West Bay; and everywhere old weather-worn benches, old stone seats, where generations of aged fishermen, with bleared eyes still as keen of sight as the eyes of shags are content to sit for hours scanning a sea and horizon familiar to them for the past seventy or eighty years.

To a boy who has explored the rocks at Portland, other rocks will be for ever dwarfed. Here are rocks large as cottages, and piled in such confusion that a child slipping through a narrow crevice may easily find himself in a secret chamber large enough for the storing of all the cheeses that a Polyphemus could husband during a period of ten years. In some of these natural caves there would be room enough for a Sea King and his debonair leman to hold high state, with fifty slippery attendants of singular but not ungraceful favour ranged around him on stools of rock, matted with seaweed.

It is best to come to the Bill when the summer visitors have dispersed to their distant homes. On a dim afternoon in November one can listen to sermons of excellent import at the foot of the pulpit rock. Thomas Hardy was aware of this or he could never have written *The Souls of the Slain.* On a winter's day the end of Portland Bill is a place of great solemnity. An eternal contest takes place here between old earth and her ancient antagonist. Year after year, century after century, millennium after millennium, it has continued, and its issue remains uncertain. All night long, with thunder and might, undaunted waves in infuriated troops hurl themselves against the indurate promontory which, whether it be daylight or pitchy darkness, remains sulky and unafraid. Meanwhile there pass by the Bill, clinging to the necks of their runaway stallions lashed to desperation by the whips of the wind, the Thuellai, women-spirits of the storm. They go shrieking over the Race. With demented outcries they scream at the four Trinity House men on the Shambles' lightship, and pass on and on above the sheer chalk headlands of the Dorset coast, until the ecstasy of their stampede at last is foiled by firm-set sensible village windows and village chimneys, and by the bare boughs of the ash, the elm, and the oak.

Who has a soul strong enough to stand alone in such a gale at the end of Portland Bill, and witness the passions of this Bedlam let loose from the dungeons of unvanquishable Nature? Man is but a shadow, a scrap of unheeded flotsam drifting we know not whither over the surface of deep waters!

DORSET CLIFF FOXES

WHEN I was in Africa it was often necessary as I pursued my duties as manager of a stock farm, to ride through a secluded valley which lay cupped under the side of an extinct crater. I used to have my Great Dane bitch running by my side. In spite of her height and strength she was by nature a nervous dog and there lived in this valley a certain jackal who discovered this fact, and as soon as we appeared the small creature would leave its cover and follow us over the plain, curling back its upper lip with the most vindictive snarls. My bitch, Egypt, after having been conducted across the open one or two times, became utterly intimidated and would always, as we approached the valley, keep close to the heels of my Somali pony. I was never able to explain the extraordinary effrontery of this particular jackal. I would sometimes try ride it down, but a few minutes after I had abandoned the chase there it would be as undaunted as ever padding persistently after us with the same malapert expression on its mask—as sour as vinegar!

Last year I was astonished in the same way by the audacity of this African beast's cousin, our English fox. It was at the end of January, the beginning of their breeding season; and one evening the garden of our cottage, hidden in an upland valley of the Dorset Downs, became a centre for the amorous contests of no less than four of these creatures. Suddenly they made us aware of their presence at dusk. I went out and sent two of them scuffling away through the cabbages. This, however, did not end matters, and during our tea, as we sat by the fire behind fast-drawn winter curtains, the clamour continued unabated. There might have been a pack of Rocky Mountain timber wolves besieging our cottage. Under the spell of their passionate rivalries they seemed to have lost their usual respect for a human habitation. When we opened the window the howls they were emitting sounded sinister. Whether the foxes were actually in the garden or somewhere in the gorse beyond the railings, I could not tell, but they were in any case very near.

I sometimes think our sea-cliff foxes do grow over-bold. Occasionally one of them is shot in a harvest field and sometimes in the winter months another may get a leg entangled in a rabbit snare and be clubbed to death by the trapper on his morning rounds, but except for such mischances they live unmolested in their deep-dug inaccessible earths cradled in safety between the blue sea and the blue sky. The knowledge that their cavernous homes, with tunnels deep sunk into the side of the precipitous cliff, have never been disturbed gives them, perhaps, more froward manners than belong to their kith who live in the Blackmore Vale, or in the water-meadows of the Frome. When an old dog fox of the cliffs, weary of his diet of rabbit bones, decides to come inland from the sea he is a rogue sturdy and most resolute to do mischief. Well versed in the marauding lore of his ancestors, husbanding in his narrow cranium the traditional tricks, the traditional expedients of his kind, I would wager a guinea that no fox in all England could match him for cunning, audacity, or adroitness. He will have one of Mr. Cobb's ganders dead before it has time to crackle out "God bless me," and throwing it across his right shoulder he will featly leap the wire of the poultry yard without so much as displacing the heavy body of the dead bird from its convenient saddle.

Not far from White Nose there is an old barn called the Sea Barn. It was built at the time of Commonwealth. The farmer thought he would keep some fowls in this lonely place. One day the lad whose task it was to shut the trap-door each evening, never came up from the hamlet. This single lapse from duty cost the farmer forty chickens, each one nicked in the neck with expert precision *for sport!*

Yet none could live long on these desolate hills without coming to love these animals. In summer they are not to be seen so often, but in the autumn months, if you walk above the "Bottoms" along the cliff paths, you are sure to catch a glimpse of one of them, curled up, perhaps, in some sheltered chalky nook enjoying the warmth of the afternoon's sun upon his red housing jacket; or with a sudden scattering of orange-coloured seeds from the pods of the stinking irises, scampering off to the cliff's edge startled by your unexpected proximity, turning at the last, with ears pricked forward, to contemplate you from the cliff's ragged rim.

Walking along the deserted stretch of beach under the promontory called Swyre Head I once noticed an odd thing—a dead rabbit and a dead fox lying side by side on the shingle killed by a fall from some dizzy ledge far above! I could understand how a rabbit suddenly surprised might in its panic tumble over, but it is a very different matter for such a miscarriage to have happened to good Master Machiavelli! It was an accident scarcely to be credited by a countryman who knows how Nature has provided this favourite child of her wild nursery with the freedom of an almost infallible insight into her duplicities. Even in the excitement of pursuit, in the excitement of escape, the judgements of foxes are uncanny in the sureness of their sagacity. In a crisis their decisions can seldom be criticised. Out of a score of alternatives they will make the one correct choice, and this without a moment's hesitation. How then can we imagine that such a wiseacre came to so gross a miscalculation with the waves sounding their menace into his long ears from four hundred feet below?

These foxes of the cliff know the seashore well. I have often seen one at low tide clambering about amongst the slippery rocks under White Nose. For the sake of a green crab they will dabble their pads in a seaweed pool or return to the sloping foot of "the landslide" with a brush soused with salt water.

One spring a vixen made use of an old earth on a slope of open downs. I noticed traces of her presence and the presence of her cubs, and getting up early one morning on the chance of enjoying the rare delight of seeing the little foxes at their play, hid myself in some near-by gorse bushes.

No living creatures could be more engaging, more winning, than are a litter of young foxes. The sun appeared over St. Aldhelm's Head sending its cold yellow rays through the long downland grasses—and sure enough, soon afterwards out came five round slate-grey cubs, one after the other, from their den. At first, grave, as was indeed befitting living creatures emerging from darkness deeper than night into a religious dawn; but after having looked about them and turned over an old bone or two, and smelt at a carline thistle—bright shining as an altar sconce—they fell naturally as children to their games of the previous evening, one jostling the other to begin their romp, then racing until all rolled over and over together. The smallest of them soon allowed its attention to be diverted from this rough and tumble by the provocative appearance of its own muffy tail, and began to whirl round and round on the soiled platform where the vixen had stretched herself out as ready to have her offspring scramble over her warm flank as to nourish them with rank fox milk from her dark nipples.

Never do I hear the husky yelp of a fox without a feeling of exultation that these darlings of Dionysus, diminutive russet wolves of the fells and fields, are still abroad in England. What a sound it is on a frosty night ringing through a bare thorn hedge behind which one of these outlaws, with slender mandibles and sensitive black nostrils, is foraging amongst the tooth-scraped roots near a sheep-fold on the chance of finding on the frozen ground of mud and flints a ewe's after-birth. Above his long cold back a myriad stars glitter; while carefully, fastidiously, and silent as Satan, he moves over the dark dreaming earth. With what easy nonchalance this bright-eyed, bright-toothed gipsy of the animal world, whose spirit can neither be tamed nor broken, filches his victuals!

One February I got my most exciting view of the intimate ways of the cliff foxes. It was a fine morning with a new soft tone in the air suggestive of the approach of spring. I thought to myself: if I walk as far as Merly Wood I may find a primrose in bud, or see a celandine in the lane showing golden at the turning where the snow lay for so long after Christmas. Instead however of going inland, I settled myself on a hidden ledge a little way down the side of a great sea headland. I knew that the guillemots would not come in for the nesting season for another six weeks, but the herring-gulls and jackdaws were glancing backwards and forwards through the crisp air above the sea, silver and shining. Suddenly far below upon a platform of loose flints, patinated white as a drift of hailstones by

Weymouth beach: not quite deserted.

Stalbridge Church.

centuries of salt sunlight, I saw two foxes making love. Over the hard floor of their selected arena there were performed a hundred mock advances, a hundred mock retreats. What a prolonged and exciting courtship it was! Sometimes the dog's pointed ears would be laid back and sometimes the vixen's. There were occasions when they would disappear under a patch of leafless elder-bushes, and then a moment later I would witness the gayest curveting, light and graceful as leaves before the wind.

When I left my position I felt as if I had been attending a religious play of classical times staged there in the morning sunshine. I might have been a spectator at a dance by the "Fox-maidens" in some vast seaside temple dedicated to the celebrations of the mysteries of Dionysus. With twitching brush, careless and gamesome, the old fox had been content to be conjured under the spell of the procreant urge; had been content to be caught away in a frenzy of body and spirit; an obedient and willing beneficiary of that rich bounty of God, under the influence of which all nature trembles and faints in its entranced worship of life.

When reference is made to a fox in mediæval literature he is almost always designated as the animal "strong in counsel," and perhaps it is the denizens of this sea-cliff colony, more than their rash and harried kinsmen of the Vale, who are to-day the worthy inheritors of this grave high-sounding title.

A CHRISTMAS TALE

NO music in the world is more beautiful than the ringing of church bells heard from a distance over an open country. At Christmas especially does this music move the spirit, so deeply associated is it with the pathos of human imaginings, the pathos of human existence. In the past the Christmas bells of Bindon Abbey must have been audible from Merly Wood to Moigne Down whenever the north-east wind blew over the waters of Poole.

It is not difficult to understand the indignation of the lay brothers and rustic farmhands who, for so long, had worked upon Abbey grounds when, at the time of the Dissolution of the Monasteries, the famous set of Bindon Bells they had heard ringing so often were distributed amongst the belfries of neighbouring parish churches. This local Catholic resentment has been eloquently preserved in the following rhyme:

"Wool streams, Coombe Wells,
Fordington cuckolds
Have a' stole
Bindon Bells."

It was in mediæval times, when Bindon Abbey was still prosperously established, that the following strange events occurred. A regular priest of the Abbey, known as Father de Brian, had interested himself in the welfare of a certain rook-boy who was employed sometimes in herding swine, and sometimes in scaring birds from the village common-field, each strip of which was divided so precisely by balks of grass. The boy was ruddy and comely to look upon, but generally thought to be one of God's innocents. His simplicity appealed to the elderly churchman who for upwards of three years gave much time to teaching the lad to read Latin from the illuminated manuscripts that were kept chained, each in its place, on the old oak reading-desks that belonged to the Abbey Library.

The monk's judgement was fully justified, and the rook-boy idiot proved an apt and industrious scholar. Not only was he taught letters, but he was also instructed in the mysteries of the Christian religion, as they were understood within the sacred walls of the Cistercian Abbey whose ruins we now look upon.

All might have gone well had not Lubberlu, for so the boy was called by the villein crofters, one May morning wandered down to the Frome. The cuckoo was bawling from the trees behind Blacknoll, and the excited river-fowl were calling to each other with amorous clucks across the floating levels of water-buttercups, that, flat and white as hail, were lying upon the surface of the clear shining stream. Then he saw a girl peering at him out of a bed of tall rushes. She was unknown to him, a maiden dressed in a coarse gown of woven flax girded with a green girdle. The two made friends. She was beautiful, but there was something fairy about her, and her voice had the shrill quality of a snipe suddenly flushed.

The two became playmates and before long lovers. It was the girl's eyes that especially bewitched the rook-boy scholar, wide-open liquid eyes that would gaze at him from under arched eyebrows. She would never tell him from what village she came, downland or heath, but always on sunshine mornings when he drove his hogs to water he would find her hidden by the swift-flowing river.

They would play together in bulrush jungles or on the open cowslip banks of the meadows, laughing to see the trout rise; and often the girl, in no Christian mood, would weave with slender fingers the field rushes into meshed cages expert to imprison a hipfrog or a dancing grasshopper.

The blue sky and the blue flowing river, the green willows and the green water-flags, together with this wild shy creature, now obsessed the whole being of Lubberlu. His listlessness became manifest. When he should have been tracing the outlines of the initial letters, bright as butterflies in the illuminated scripts of the Abbey, he would be looking out of the narrow lancet window in the direction of the water meadows. For many weeks the old priest held his peace, but as the summer grew towards its close and the last loads of the yellow harvest had been stored in the great ivy-covered Grange, he pressed the boy to make his confession. When he had finished the old man stood up, and with tears running down his cheeks made the sign of the blessed cross over the straw-coloured head of his conjured pupil. He suspected this wanton daughter of the river of belonging to a family outside of Middle Earth—at best a river nymph owning no mortal soul.

After the evening of his confession Lubberlu was never able to find his darling again. All through the autumn in the dusk of late afternoons he would trace the banks of the Frome in its winter desolation, calling and calling from Wool Bridge to Moreton Ford.

At Christmas it fell out that it was the old Priest's turn to officiate at early morning Mass in the small chapel at Ringstead. To reach the village at the appointed hour it was necessary to arouse the porter while it was still night. Lubberlu was to act as acolyte and was already blowing on his fingers outside the gateway of the Abbey. The two started away under the bright stars—the priest on a grey mule, the boy walking at his side. The hedge grass was crisp with hoar-frost. They left the wide, white drove above Belhuish and struck across by Dagger's Gate to the Roman Road that runs above the cliffs. On the downs, in the lew of the furzen, they came upon a flock of sheep, the peaceful animals with frosted backs of wool lying on the stiff turf about the Merlin thorn in an enchanted circle. The venerable clerk did not fail to remind the boy of the scene on the hills of Bethlehem and of the blinding vision that had come to the chatting shepherds.

The homestead dwellers of Ringstead had always been obstinate sons of Belial. Was it for this reason that they and their dwellings were so soon to be destroyed by pirates? They gained a scant livelihood by fishing and it may be that their hours under the stars sharpened their wits to ask awkward questions. How did it come about that Norman priests, like stags in the pride of their grease, knew so much more than ordinary churls? Had they ever spoken with a dead man risen out of the grave?

These jolly libertine lobster catchers had spent their

Christmas Eve feasting and love-making behind the doors of their thatched mud houses, that windowless and chimneyless resembled so many beehives set in rows each side of the stream, the very stream that still flows through Ringstead Wood. Much brawn of tusked swine they had devoured, swilling it down with draughts of strong mead. The sound of the small chapel bell, of the Gabriel bell, echoed through the wood, sharp as the tinkling of an icicle in the morning air. The fisher folk snored on in their darkened hovels. None came to the small church, the chancel arch of which is to be seen to-day built about by the wall of the woodland cottage. With my own fingers I have traced its mouldings, the very mouldings which that morning received upon their surfaces the flickering light from the altar candles, a yellow light shining between the beech-trees, visible beyond the seaweed rocks.

The rest of the ancient Ringstead legend is best told in the form of the Christmas ballad which has preserved the sequel of the story in a kind of antiphonal chant talking place between the holy priest and this love-lost son of the earth:

"Boy:—

Green were her eyes—yellow were her eyes—
Her eyes were like withered sedge!

Priest:—

This is holy Mass and the hour flies
And there is red in the churchyard hedge,
Raise me aloft my taper's flame,
Light me my candles three,
For I must call on the Baby's name
Who is born to young Mary.

Boy:—

O father, I see a blood-red streak
In the reeds where first I caught her—
And I hear a cry makes my heart weak—
And turns my bones to water.
The marsh-bittern and lone curlew,
That cry comes not from them.

Priest:—

Bring me bread and wine, my Lubberlu
And hold my vestment's hem!
The candles burn—the oxen kneel.
Boy, bring me my holy book—
Born is the King of Israel!

Boy:—

Oh, father, my father, look!
She is pressing her face 'gainst the window-pane,
Where the saints stare in a row,
And her lips are red with the morning's stain,
And her cheeks are white like snow!

Priest:—

'Tis Christmas morn and the Mass unsung
For the Baby of young Mary!

* * *

But the idiot boy from his side had sprung.
At the window prone was he.
And the oxen knelt in their frozen shed
And the sheep in the hurdled pen;
But Lubberlu lay stark and dead,
He never will come again.

* * *

They sign his breast and they sign his brow
With the cross to which they pray—
But two lost souls are flying now
Over the reeds and over the snow,
Over the hills and away."

EASTER IN DORSET

OF all the great Church festivals none is so full of grace as is the festival of Easter. It is possible that the indescribable feeling of gladness that passes over the green acres of Europe at this season of the year is really and truly derived from the Catholic doctrine of the resurrection. To Christian men and women whose hearts have been broken by the deaths of their mothers or fathers or children or lovers an occasion that celebrates this central dogma of their faith could hardly fail to proffer—so comfortable are its words—a deep psychic release. If a religious faith had been evolved with no obligation than to satisfy the innocent longings of the human heart it could hardly have fallen upon a doctrine more reassuring than that the actual bodies of those we love should rise again from the lonely grave in glorified forms. Indeed it is almost impossible for an intelligent mind not to experience some slight apprehension lest this celebrated Christian hope may not err a little on the side of complacence, so far does it exceed our deserts and overleap the boundaries of our most sanguine forecast.

Apart, however, from the supernatural dispensations provided so easily by conventional creeds, there are other reasons that may to some extent explain the happiness of simple people at this time of the year.

The Venerable Bede, one of the most lovable and learned characters in Church History, instructs us that the word Easter, like the names of the days of the week, is a survival from the old Teutonic mythology, being taken from the name given to the Nordic month corresponding with our April, a month dedicated to the Anglo-Saxon Goddess of spring time—Eostre or Ostara. With such a derivation in mind it is easy to understand how to many people the stricter sacerdotal persuasions may, with little difficulty, become merged in a less self-conscious feeling of natural worship. A profound unaffected gratitude, atavistic, marrow-deep, for the return of the vernal equinox, is an emotion shared by all. It can be taken from us by no exacting pontifical claims. It is a universal inheritance. In a very remote period men were competent to mark the turning back of the sun at the time of the winter solstice, a turning back which after the waning of three or four moons revived once more in the vegetable world the leap of procreant life. This gladness at the dead earth's re-awakening, at the reappearance of the "corn spirit," has been embodied in many a wild and beautiful myth. In ancient days, about the Mediterranean basin this natural sensibility was present in the cults of Attis, Adonis, Dionysus, and Osiris. The priests of this last religion were accustomed in the spring to perform a ritual of searching for the dead God, and finding him alive, would cry: "We have found him. Let us rejoice." In their wisdom the Church Fathers were careful not to discourage these heathen modes of passionate piety, but to turn them towards their own Paschal mysteries. Sir James Frazer, who has brought so much light to the study of the origins of human religions, writes as follows: "Taken altogether the coincidences of Christian with heathen festivals are too close and too numerous to be accidental. They mark the compromise which the church in the hour of its triumph was compelled to make with its vanquished but still dangerous rivals."

I feel a certain satisfaction in remembering that the Christian churches reflect a worship so simple, so ancient, and so easy to be understood. Sottish indeed would that man be who could not find it in his heart to rejoice on a fine spring morning. It is then more than at any other time of the year that the appeal of the visible world falls most insistently upon us. In April and May there is not a bird that does not sing in thrilling notes of the ecstasy of love. Above White Nose, above the White Horse, above High Stoy, above Hell Stones the throats of crested larks swell beneath tiny feathers as they vibrate with unpremeditated rapture in the high ethereal levels of our planet's atmosphere. And while these mote-like birds, far up in a crystal heaven, blue as the blue in a child's paint-box strain to give expression to their dancing passion, lords and ladies in every hedge unfold their privileged spears, purple and pale, and golden dandelions sustained by sap, white as the milk of elfin dairy cows, bring confidence to the work-a-day, turnpike ditches. If compassion for men's broken lives was the most important word uttered by Jesus of Nazareth, we have but to listen to the nightingale that each year nests in Holworth spinney troubling the dreaming heads of Nelly, Bessie, and Betty Parker, and of other mortals living in that lovely valley, which of all in Dorset is first to welcome the spring.

The country tokens that I myself especially associate with the Easter holidays are five in number: the pussy willows that we in England use to represent the fan-shaped palm leaves which were strawed in the way when Christ made his heroic entrance into Jerusalem; the loping gambols of long-hipped hares over dry fields of sprouting corn; the eggs of hedge-sparrows, in size and colour so fascinating to the æsthetic taste of children; short-stemmed scented white violets; and, finally, primroses with their faint tremulous smell that possesses "a kind of tragic intensity."

In Matthew Arnold's romantic poem, "The Forsaken Merman," it is the sound of Easter bells reaching even to the deep sea caves that vexes the sea king's willing lady to the remembrance of her mortal soul:

"Once she sate with you and me,
On a red-gold throne in the heart of the sea,
And the youngest sate on her knee.
She comb'd its bright hair, and she tended it well,
When down swung the sound of a far-off bell.
She sigh'd, she look'd up through the clear green sea;
She said: 'I must go, for my kinsfolk pray
In the little grey church on the shore to-day.
'Twill be Easter-time in the world—ah me!
And I lose my poor soul, Merman! here with thee.'"

Perhaps we are justified in believing that it was not only for the sake of "the priest, and the bell and the holy well" that this girl found it in her heart to desert her little Mermaiden with bright hair and cold strange eyes; perhaps we may also attribute her faithlessness to a sudden drowning memory of the beauty of lanes and fields and woods at this time of the year, when glossy preoccupied rooks in their swaying attics sit close upon their blotched eggs, and heaths are "starr'd with brume," and the whole of England is a green land of fairie, and all the county of Dorset a "garden of Adonis."

DORCHESTER CHARACTERS

FOR many decades I had observed with sympathy a particular porter on the platform of the Great Western Railway at Dorchester. He was a short man wearing a square black beard and there had always seemed to be something about him kindly and unaggressive. As the years went by grievous old age came upon this porter until a time when, scan the station as I might, I saw him no more. It had always been my intention to talk with him and ask him whether he remembered my father at the time when he had lived at Dorchester, but this I had never done fearing to embarrass him. Now that his familiar figure was not to be seen I regretted my reserve, and inquiring for his address discovered it to be on the Bridport Road in one of the houses of the row facing the allotments. Postponing my immediate affairs I walked to the house and soon found myself being generously entertained by the old porter and his wife, both of whom remembered my father very well indeed. I left there my mind full of the record of this good man's years. I seemed to see his life spread out before me—the innumerable excursion trains that he must have ushered through Dorchester on their way to Weymouth, the endless stream of travellers that he must have helped, involving himself for the price of a few coppers in their self-interested anxieties; and the hours also that were his own spent for the most part in his allotment plot; for he assured me he was very fond of gardening, adding that his shallots and broad beans had always been well showing before the winter was over. Indeed as he spoke I almost came to share with him the troubling beauty of those far off February twilights, when the evenings of the 'eighties and the evenings of the 'nineties were beginning to lengthen out, and he would lean upon his spade to listen to the blackbird's liquid note coming to him from the leafless hedge with so tremulous a sound that the very inmates of the nearby workhouse must have been happy for a moment with their memories, as they sat drinking their Government tea, a trifle "on the thin side," out of mugs of white china. How dutiful the old man was, how humble—and yet how self respecting, devoted to his ordained duties as those generous cart-horses are who never require the whip, but will fall dead rather than seem to fail their masters however heavy their loads.

The last time I was in Dorchester, some fifteen months ago, I gave myself the present of a weed basket. The basket shop stood almost opposite Foot's, the seed merchant. The daughter of the house served me. As I was leaving she said: "I have often seen you pass down the street and wondered whether you were not one of the sons of the Rev. C. F. Powys. You look like him." She could not have said anything that pleased me better. I could almost see my father's tall figure going by outside with the long strides that were so characteristic of his walk. Although I am so proud that Dorchester is my native town I can remember nothing of it in the days of my infancy, having been carried into Somerset some time during the second year of my life. Changes, however, are apt to come slowly in the old Roman city, and I understand that the gentleman who succeeded my father at Rothesay House forty-eight years ago still resides there. I now began to ask about the woman's own father and she told me that he had spent his whole life at his trade of weaving willow slivers from the rivers Frome and Stour into shapes and receptacles useful to the daily needs of mortal life. She showed me baskets of every size and design—huge baskets for the bakers and light osier cages for carrying roses wet with June rains into the airy halls of the vicarages and manor houses of Dorset. "And where is your father now?" I asked. "He is dying overhead," she answered simply. "They are proposing to widen the street, and we have to move, and the thought of leaving the old house has been a trouble to him. We expected that he would have died last night." Her words proved only too true for the next day I read in the *Dorset Echo* an account of the octogenarian's death. Unfortunately I have been prevented from visiting Dorchester since that day. I understand the old man's son still carries on the trade of his father in a side street, and nobody who loves the county and appreciates the value of sound handicrafts should fail to search him out so that his primitive art may not be allowed to decline.

With my new purchase under my arm I now entered Boon's shop. Here it was that I experienced a less fortunate encounter. A large, fashionably-dressed woman had followed me in and immediately began making her domineering presence felt amongst us. I knew her type well. She was one of those "new Dorset ladies" whose breath is withering to everything that is free and charming in life. Chance had but lately compelled me to spend an hour in the house of one of these people and from where I had sat I could overhear three of them "with varnished faces" conversing on a sofa. They were talking of the trouble they experienced with their domestic servants. It distressed me that simple Dorset maidens from happy villages perhaps under the protection of the Bond family, or of the Weld family, should be suddenly caught away, to find themselves in the power of these "roving Griffs or Harpies dread." Why cannot these pretentious women learn from the old-fashioned rulers of Dorset whose company they so covet that to belong to a family that has been "gentle" for centuries should be equivalent to accepting a moral responsibility for the happiness and ease of every human soul that crosses our path during our few years of earth existence? The way this particular lady treated the men behind the counter was scarcely to be borne—the harsh timbre of her voice, void of all human feeling, the cold "frightfulness" of her eye, so devastating to the life of the spirit!

How eagerly I crossed the road to refresh myself with the jocund personality of my old acquaintance, Barney Hallet the scissors grinder, who every Wednesday and Saturday is to be found in his wheeled house a little beyond the entrance to the Town Hall. This man, as was his father before him, has been stationed near to St. Peter's church for time out of mind. The old man, so it is rumoured, used to drive his diminutive caravan into Dorchester by steam power. He may have been an engineering genius, but I am sure his skill with blunt cutlery never excelled that of his son. Dressed as a cyclist, for in his day (he is now past three score years and ten) Mr. Barney Hallet was a great performer "on the wheel," he will hop lightly out of his "house" to accept all orders, as merry as a glossy white-epauletted male chaffinch: "I have come down this fine morning to pick up a round piece of grain O!"

We had been shown once a rag rug made by men in the Dorchester prison and had always wanted to possess one. One afternoon several years ago I decided to make enquiries about them at the Dorchester Gaol. I entered the drive and presently stood before the great gates. I rang a bell and immediately heard the sound, which in mediæval times must have been so familiar, of a porter's slow movements and the clank and clang of sliding bolts and bars. I was almost immediately reassured, however, by the porter's appearance—a typical Dorset policeman, a man from the fields, firm and of powerful build, but above everything good-natured. He was, I think, puzzled by the unexpected nature of my talk. "His Honour the Governor might know," he ventured, but it was evident he had no intention of taking upon himself the least responsibility in so frivolous a matter. It now happened that I saw a figure far away in the interior of the building of "iron bars and cement" advancing towards us. "There is someone coming," I said. The policeman swung round. "The Governor his own self," he said sternly, and without another word let the great door close, leaving me outside to contemplate a notice of the penalties to fall upon the head of anyone rash enough to help a friend to escape. Curiosity overcame my diffidence and prompted me still to loiter in the prison grounds as might an importunate beggar. I was rewarded by being given a chance to put my question to the Governor. If I had felt at ease with the man I felt still more at ease with the master. The gentleman who was at that time acting as Governor of Dorchester Prison appeared to me to be completely without those affectations of self-importance that so often render the presence of eminent officials insupportable to ordinary people. He was a sensitive man, and an extremely civilised man. I would have trusted him to solve the most complicated human situation "seasoning Justice with Mercy."

For a long time I have realised that a period of panic might unite the forces of the authorative religions with the forces of property. The Sedition Bill, recently promulgated, if it had been passed by Parliament, would have provided the nervous dominant classes with a weapon more dangerous than any that has been devised since the notorious "Gagging Acts" of Lord Sidmouth. There remain also on the Statute Books slumbering laws always ready to be revived in hours of prejudice and superstition. A vacation in "this den" would no longer now alarm me, in this den so honoured by the names of George Loveless, Richard Carlile, and Wakefield. Wakefield whiled away his period of confinement here by exchanging Latin verses with Charles James Fox.

Certain country towns are so romantic in themselves that simply to be walking in their streets seems a high privilege. This especially is the case with Dorchester. In the days when Barney Hallet's "family coach" was allowed a curb station in the High Street under the shadow of St. Peter, I have often stepped by it on a spring morning to admire the greenness of the Stinsford water meadows as seen at the end of the London Road. I have looked at them with nostalgia thinking how in the ditches the first cuckoo flowers must be in bud. Few capital towns can afford a view so soothing to the mind in its moments of infirmity. One behind the other, there they stand, the great timbered trees of Mellstock, sheltering by their presence all the garnered associations of Thomas Hardy's long lifetime.

However, without doubt, Dorchester is most completely Dorchester not in the spring but in the winter. Oh! how happy I have been shopping in this town on the Saturday before Christmas. The thronging crowds afford then a liberal education as to the inner being of the county—the eighteenth-century country faces of the farmers, homely and hearty, as they stand in crowds outside the Antelope, "their talk being" of bullocks: the face of a farm labourer almost religious in its refinement, glimpsed for a moment as the man passes along the pavement with a sprig of holly in his cap. To be abroad in Dorchester on a Christmas Eve is an experience never to be forgotten. By half-past three, with the first snow of the year fluttering down, the shops are brightly lighted. The streets offer many a lively scene—the cottage woman, over-burdened with parcels and with young-eyed children one, two, and three all clinging to the folds of her round skirt; the town girl light of step with a present for her true love; the aged upstair lodger, his misery forgot, glad to have been about in the taverns Christmassing and with silver still in his trouser pockets; the genial fishwife, my own friend, at her place, with two heaps piled up on her wide wooden tray, the one of silver, the other of gold—for see how her fat fresh herrings shine silver bright, her oranges from Spain like a pyramid of brass! The casual, friendly, country people move up and down. Barney Hallet, because of the snow, either shuts tight his door or begins to trundle his house away before him, like an agile unedible snail moving itself backwards out of an unsympathetic environment. The gipsy child, born the previous August in a barley field, clasps her brown hands to see the snowflakes, white goose feathers of softest down. Her mother enfolds her with her shawl and nods to the boy with the mistletoe. It is time to move into the shelter of the favoured haunt well out of the way of official scrutiny. I remember just such a Christmas Eve and how I enjoyed riding back to Chaldon in good Mr. Goult's van. I remember his stopping by a white field-gate to let a mother and her three children out into the winter night, and how relieved the woman was, and we all were, to hear the voice of the husband who had evidently attended to his farm horses early so as to be in time to guide his family across the fields and over the tall stile under the elm-tree, and how as the rest of us were rolled forward towards the Red Lion I could not but envisage the homecoming of our late companions; the carter encouraged to sit down in the familiar chair by the fire, while preparations for tea were in progress, with the children's voices raised over one of the afternoon's adventures or persistently calling out in excited anticipation for the morrow. Almost I could hear the goodman tell, as with grave preoccupation he removed one heavy boot after the other, how "proper keen" it had been "out on the grounds" that morning.

Then our turn came and down we had to get with many a "Good night all" heard through the darkness across Chaldon

Stalbridge: the old rectory.

Stinsford Church, where the heart of Thomas Hardy lies buried.

The Cobb, Lyme Regis.

Tolpuddle: the cottage where the martyrs held their trade union meetings.

Green. A walk of a mile and a half over the down was now before me and I recollect well how, as I reached the foot of Chalky Knap, with my mind full of old Christmasses at home, an inclination to worship came suddenly upon me, and in gratitude for having been alive again in Dorchester on such a night I did in the darkness give utterance to the only prayer that in the disobedience of my heart I ever use. "That it may please Thee to have mercy upon all men."

WEST BOTTOM

THERE are occasions when religious feeling will suddenly take possession of the most obdurate spirit. It happened so with me three weeks ago as I watched out the Old Year. Suddenly the sound of bells came drifting over downs stiff and ashen white with hoar-frost. In the sound were all the romantic associations of mediæval piety. The moon was shining and in her white, cold, beautiful light I knew that there was rising from the pastures of every English shire, far up into the wintry heavens, this wonderful crystal music familiar in the time of our fathers and in the old times before them. Every separate grass-blade, every single twig in the thornhedges, and the top bar of each field-gate was glittering, and over the frozen plough-lands covered with flints came the tumbling rhythm of the belfry changes, now loud, now faint, as though caught upon the wind from a wedding procession taking place far away on the other side of the distant hills, where by some enchantment spring was already, with yellow daffodils and yellow primroses strewing the path of true lovers happy at last.

I knew that on that night the whole of Dorset was lying under the spell of the moon. With an influence strong enough to draw the sea high up the shelving banks of the Chesil Beach, the radiance of this mysterious dead planet was spread over the country. It was upon the stonework of Hardy's Monument; it was upon the dove-cot attic above the great nave of Sherborne Abbey; it was upon the feathered bodies of dreaming Abbotsbury swans, and upon the shining horns of the winter-coated heifers recumbent upon Batcombe Downs, their heavy breathing visibly bringing warmth to the midnight air of High Stoy.

Behind this old-world music of the Lulworth bells there was audible at regular intervals a sound as deep-throated as the respiration of a dragon. It is rumoured that the prophet Daniel once silence a Babylonian dragon with a diet of hair and pitch—but where is the thaumaturge who can bring repose to the restless sea which for millenniums beyond the computation of man has been subject to the treacherous charm of the moon?

It is not only through the sense of hearing that the imagination can be stirred to a heightened consciousness of earth existence. From time out of mind certain localities have been renowned for evoking moods of spiritual awareness. In ancient days when a cultivated Roman approached some place where the natural scenery was particularly solemn and impressive—a mountain gorge or a forest glade—it was his custom to utter in the form of a grace these words: "Numen in est," "Deity is in this place."

Of such places of worship in Dorset I think none is more awe-inspiring than that portion of the coast known to fishermen and rabbit-catchers as West Bottom. It is the first of the Bottoms between White Nose and Lulworth walking eastward that drops away to the sheer cliff's edge. Its sloping sides are so steep and so slippery that nobody inclined to giddiness should venture down them. Far below on the very edge of the dizzy cliff is a diminutive spinney of weather-stunted alder-trees, and to the right rises the Fountain Rock, a squared column of chalk banded with flints, and of such enormous proportions that it could, I believe, without strain or displacement support the whole weight of Salisbury Cathedral. This Cyclopean pillar of native marble rises straight up from the level of the beach below to tower high above the cup of this downland valley.

Even in summer weather, when butterflies are everywhere, fritillaries and chalk-hill blues and Lulworth skippers, West Bottom remains a desolate place. Many a time have I disturbed a fox there and sent it hustling away to its inaccessible earth halfway down the precipice. Many a time, attracted by the shrill cry of the peregrine falcon, I have witnessed the death of a carrier-pigeon as, tired of wing, it was flying homewards to its familiar backyard loft in Weymouth. Two other birds, the cormorant and the raven, both of them fowls of ill omen to man from earliest times, are frequently to be seen flying in this undisturbed place. And yet if boy or girl, old man or old woman heavy of heart, and impatient of human comforters, wishes to bow before the knees of Nature, the stern mother of us all, they could do not better than to visit West Bottom.

No vexations connected with the follies of society could torment the mind of one standing alone in this awful temple not made with hands. Anxieties deriving from worldly preoccupations could not but weigh lightly here, where the facile spirit in its habitation of bones is nursed in the lap of these noble hills. "As the race of leaves so the race of man is," wrote Homer. To us the Fountain Rock appears as a foundation stone of eternity, and yet in the eyes of God it is but yesterday that its substance was cemented together out of crushed shells from the sea's floor. We are nurtured in illusions. Which of us has a soul firm enough to understand the crying of the winds or to construe the words of the waves?

CORFE CASTLE

WHEN I was living in New York City with my fortunes at a low ebb, it was my custom to breakfast every morning at a popular restaurant in Seventh Avenue. The noise of the heavy drays thundering by in the direction of the Battery, the distant rumble of the elevated railway, in fact, the whole stir of the great city's life, so audible in the cheap eating house, would often be to me extremely depressing.

It happened that one day among the English mail that I had brought in with me to read I found a *Dorset Daily Echo*. I opened the paper, and the very first thing that caught my eye was a communication from someone living in Wyke Regis, saying that on a certain early date in April he had observed a cuckoo sitting on the top of Sandsfoot Castle and calling, or, as we say in Dorset, halloing at the top of his voice.

This chance paragraph filled me with an overwhelming home-sickness. I could envisage the scene so clearly—a sunny April morning with the daffodils in every Weymouth garden swaying in the crisp seaside air, and with the cuckoo, its tail uptilted, fresh returned from the forests of the Congo, perched for a moment on the summit of one of the four walls of the old fort, its heart as merry as the sunshine.

Sandsfoot Castle was the castle of my very earliest recollections, and although in actual fact it represents a late example of this mediæval form of defence, it has always seemed to me to possess a singular personality of its own, a personality as simple and as solid as that of the "castle" on a chessboard, standing firm in its corner and amid other more sophisticated pieces.

Of course, I soon realised that Corfe Castle was of far greater historic interest; indeed, that it was "the most romantic castle in the world," and truly I have never yet seen any other castle that has caused me to revise this judgement.

How magnificent this massed grey pile of heavy stones can

look, with its tall keep still dominating the valleys to the north and to the south between the green downs of the Island of Purbeck!

What native of Dorchester, of Weymouth, of Wareham, or of Poole does not feel his imagination awakened when out of the window of a Southern Railway carriage he catches a glimpse for a moment of this familiar Dorset momument, its outline appearing like the dog-teeth in the skull of a dead wolf?

The late Mr. Herbert Weld once told me that when the King of France first caught sight of Lulworth Castle he exclaimed "*C'est La Bastille*," and nobody could deny that the remains of the civilised pleasure house of this ancient Catholic family would even today, from a superficial point of view, justify the royal foreigner's quip, though except for its mural façade the Frenchman's exclamation might have been better applied to Corfe—with its grim insistent traditions of bloodshed and oppression!

In March, when the first white violets begin to show in the hedgerow banks of the Bloody Road, the mind easily reverts to the old story of the high-born girl out of Devonshire, whose eccentric habit it was to chastise her son with long wax candles so that he, Ethelred, even when King of England, could never abide these ecclesiastical symbols.

Attractive she must have been for it was for love of her that the King's henchman betrayed his master and forfeited his life; and froward she must have been, with a frowardness that culminated at last in the "foulest evil ever committed by the English since they came to Britain"—the cry of a murdered King! and the tragic clattering of a horse's hoofs! "And she wente to the Kynge and welcumed hym with fayne and blandishing wordes, and commanded to fetch bred and wyne to the Kynge—and wyles ye Kynge dranke ye boteler toke a knyfe and roof ye Kynge through ye body to ye herte."

Today the race of jackdaws, with bright eyes and black, dusty, sunshine-smelling feathers, inhabit the dizzy ledges of the castle, where the same stones retain the same positions that they held when the voice of the worst of the Plantagenets sounded through the halls, the voice of John Lackland returned from hunting the tall deer, and calling for his meat.

It was here that Prince Arthur's sister, Eleanor, the Damsel of Botagne, was for a long time imprisoned. Scarcely in the whole range of our island's history can we find a more terrible indictment than the one written by a contemporary chronicler of the cunning and passionate King—"Foul as it is, hell itself is defiled by the fouler presence of John."

I have an odd recollection that has to do with Corfe. My brother Theodore many years ago was looking for East Chaldon, that is to say, for a quiet, peaceful, hidden-away Dorset village, where he could spend the days of his life in surroundings harmonious to the grave temper of his mind.

We were coming back from visiting Kimmeridge, and late in the evening of a lovely spring day entered Corfe to find the space before the inn crowded with people listening to an orator who was speaking from his carriage. We had not been aware that any election was in progress, and stood for a moment to enjoy the spectacle in the twilight.

It is as dangerous a thing to catch the eye of a politician as that of a drunkard, and almost immediately after our appearance we realised to our embarrassment that this prospective Liberal candidate for South Dorset had stepped from his brougham and was making his way directly towards us. A moment later he was shaking our hands with infatuated cordiality. My brother, a natural philosopher, is not easily put out by unexpected happenings, and it was not long before, with characteristic suavity, he had extricated us from our ambiguous position.

Another visit, scarcely less happy in retrospect, occurred a few years later when I examined the ruins with my brother's two boys. We learned the names of the Buttavant and Plunkenet Towers, and also we observed how the main streets of the village converge upon the ancient centre of importance—the castle gates! I remember we looked up at the two guardrobe shafts, still a conspicuous part of the masonry on the south side of the keep. These guard-robes, or ancient indoor retiring closets, acquired their name from the prevailing practice of hanging up the more valuable household furs in them, it being imagined that strong odours secured the garments against depredations from the moth that corrupts.

When I visited Durenstein a few years ago I was surprised to find that the castle where Richard Cœur de Lion was imprisoned resembled Corfe very closely. It stands on a hill of much the same size and height, and its forlorn ruins give to a traveller the same impression of the disasters of long ago. Perhaps during the months of his bitter incarceration, before Blondel, his minstrel, found him, the thoughts of the heroic, magnanimous King sometimes turned to his own similar fortification in the west of England, where his brother may very well have been at the same time plotting subtly against him. True it is that there is no river near Corfe, and even if nature had caused the Frome to flow through this break in the Purbeck Hills it could never have appeared as impressive as does the Danube sweeping by the little Austrian village on its way to the Black Sea.

HEROES OUT OF THE PAST

TWO or three years ago I had occasion to enter the furniture shop of Hawk and Freeman in Weymouth. My wants were attended to by an active middle-aged man of ruddy countenance. He was not tall, but his athletic carriage and the huge breadth of his chest declared him to be a man of great bodily strength. As Wordsworth phrases it, he might have danced "from head to foot equipt in iron mail." When at the conclusion of my business I gave my name he asked me tentatively if I was not related to L. C. Powys the old Rugby-football player. In a flash I understood now why I had so admired this man's physique. He was Marshall, a member of the famous team of forwards which had won so much honour for the county of Somerset at the beginning of the century.

These men had been the heroes of my boyhood—Marshall, S. M. J. Wood, John Daniel, L. C. Powys, H. T. Gamlin, "Buster" Soane, Brice, and, above all, G. M. Carey who had captained Oxford and afterwards became a far-famed international champion. How I used to follow their achievements in the pages of the *Sportsman*, and how thrilled I once was to see a photograph of my brother Littleton in the *Sporting and Dramatic* standing in a "line out" when he was playing in a trial match for the South of England! Some school "blood" who had the privilege of reading the house papers at his *leisure* before ever we small fry were allowed so much as a snatched glance at them would suddenly look across at me and say: "Well! Powys Minor, I see your brother did pretty well against Cornwall"; and these condescending words would send an indescribable glow of delight through all my marrow-bones, such as no success of my own or any of my brother's has ever succeeded in making me experience since. Heroes of an afternoon in rain and mud, heroes of an hour, heroes of the football field, terrible as a pride of lions, swift as forest stags, magnificent in the glory of young manhood—the passing of thirty or more years has carelessly scattered you like leaves before a winter's wind. Many of you are already dead and buried; others with stiffening joints living in blameless obscurity—your feats forgotten, your celebrated names that once sounded trumpet calls to the ears of half the population of England, scarce so much as heard of by the present generation of sportsmen.

These reflections, especially a memory of "John" Carey in the spring of his years, brought back to my mind a particularly happy holiday walk I had taken with my brother, John Cowper, across country from Montacute to Sherborne. Our way lay through the village of Thorne Coffin, and from there we struck over the fields until we came to the banks of the River Yeo a little above Mudford. It had been our intention to avoid the roads. We had imagined that we would find a footbridge or a bridle-bridge somewhere between Mudford and Pen Mill. The Yeo here divides the county of Somerset from the county of Dorset. We followed the river's crooked course through endless sun-dried meadows, but never a bridge did we come upon. It was the month of August, and under the blaze of noon, even the dark green leaves of the alders appeared to faint in the heat. We passed several drinking-places for cattle, but always the water was too deep for wading. When the beautiful firmly-built spire of Trent Church came into view across the fields on the opposite side of the river our patience became exhausted.

In those days it was my mother's custom one morning in every month to substitute for our regular after-breakfast Bible-reading a close study of certain missionary papers. The most arresting of these journals was called *The Gleaner*. In one of its issues there had been a picture of two missionaries swimming across a crocodile river with their clothes tied to their heads. I now suggested to my brother, though he was my elder by twelve years, that we should do the same. Using his belt to bind his garments to his head, an imitation of my memory of the picture, he boldly pushed off from the bank, while I, but a little shaveling missionary, swam in his wake. He had almost reached the further shore when his head-gear grew suddenly unbalanced, and like some pyramidical turban toppled with a dull splash into the dark water "of the River Lunt." For a moment I thought the bundle was destined never to be recovered but would float down-stream until it became an object of casual interest to loiterers on Ilchester Bridge. Avoiding as best I could the backwash of the disaster, for my brother in his efforts to recover his clothing floundered and splashed like an amphibious dragon ducking for his mate, I managed by a prudent deviation from my direct course to bring my own small parcel of goods safe to land. My brother's clothes were saturated, as were his boots. There came from them also the unmistakable odour of the breath of eels and the abdomens of river fishes. We decided it would be best to hurry forward to Sherborne hoping that the hard exercise would prevent him from catching cold. I remember that there were autumn crocuses, or "naked nannies," blooming everywhere in the fields, a flower I had never seen before, but we were too perturbed to take much note of them.

Up the lovely Trent lanes we went, perhaps the most lovely hazel-nut lanes to be found in all Dorset, until we reached the valley field with beech-trees growing on its summit, trees to which my brother Bertie and I would come during the intolerable deserts of term-time so that we could refresh our spirits by looking across Yeovil to where in the mid-distance, reduced to the scale of a fairy landscape, would appear the outlines of Ham Hill, of Hedgecock, of Montacute Hill, of the Scotch Firs, and of Odcombe Ridge, outlines that never failed to bring tears to our eyes so associated were they with the days of happy freedom. There we knew in the familiar village, with its tall church, its Abbey Gateway, and its Borough, our father, so utterly unlike any schoolmaster, was going in and out of the cottage doors of his parish, and after enjoying his walk in the late afternoon returning punctually to his family tea, a strong, baffling, nay, seemingly invincible safeguard against all the vulgarities and miseries that we had learned to connect with the outside world.

At last we were coming down Cheap Street with water still oozing from my brother's boots at every step he took. No urchins in all Dorset have sharper ears or quicker eyesight for detecting the ludicrous than do those of this ancient Abbey town. Instantaneously it was rumoured that strangers, and none of the grandest, were advancing down the street. In my heart I prayed fervently that the manner of our entrance would never be reported to the scoffers and mockers of the Wilson's House day-room. We had now reached the corner opposite Ford's tuck-shop. There was a seed-shop here, and when he first came to Sherborne as a schoolmaster, "John" Carey used to lodge above this shop. As we arrived at the corner a carriage drew up in front of us. Out of this carriage stepped Mr. Carey with his Scottish bride. There they stood before us, the man and maid whose life together was to be so happy, so fruitful, so momentous for the character of Sherborne School. Not less noble, not less radiant must the youthful Achilles have appeared when first he led his darling Briseis "of the fair cheeks" to his tent, in the bright sunlight of antiquity. This "hero" John had always been fascinated by the personality of my eldest brother, "Prester" John. They had been at school together, and there had existed some strange affinity between the Sir Galahad King of the playing-fields and the Welsh Merlin King of "enchanted grounds." It was an alliance between an eagle and "a plumed serpent." True Guernsey gentleman that Mr. Carey was he introduced us to his lady without showing by a flicker that there was anything out of the ordinary in having encountered a friend in the town's main street as wet and dripping as a merman from the sea! In after years he would remind me of the meeting which had for all four of us, I think, a peculiar significance, as though we had been allowed for a single moment to stand together on life's golden threshold with complete awareness.

We now walked to Dingley's, the popular haberdasher, and there my brother bought a ready-made suit. This ready-made suit he used to wear for many years. It pleased him to be reminded of our adventure. I liked the suit for the same reason and also because it was bought at Dingley's. Old Mr. Dingley had for a long time played an important part in my meditations upon life. He had become a prominent figure in my boyhood's mythology. From the dormitory windows at the Preparatory

School I had often seen the old gentleman taking pleasure in his beautiful garden of Netherton. On Sunday mornings in the summer time, when "the first bell" had rung, I would observe him already up, strolling through his paddock or opening the door of his glass grape-house, a quiet old gentleman soberly dressed in black. As soon as ever they heard the click of the small wicket-gate, his two "perfect" Jersey milch-cows would come up to him, and I would then see him touch their cool muzzles with his cuffed hands and presently begin to stroke their foreheads as though he wished to bless their simplicity.

It was always painful to me when any portion of this garden life of the good old man was made common by the derisive observations of my companions. I never wanted them even so much as to discover the names of the two dairy cows, "Moonshine" and "Cowslip," still less, as they let the striped holland blind rush up with a hideous click, to hear them say in a contemptuous tone. "There is that old ass Dingley walking in his garden as usual."

These sloping lawns and buttercup paddocks of Netherton must have ministered in a very deep way to the pure spirit of the old Nonconformist tradesman. To observe his grave figure moving with so tranquil a step, so religiously, amongst his flower-beds, was to be initiated into the secret of a profound peace. The cool shady spaces of Netherton made him, perhaps, think of the land of Beulah, in *The Pilgrim's Progress*, where travellers to celestial city were encouraged to linger a little at the end of their journeying; so he now, at the end of his long life, unmolested by the noisy preoccupations of commerce, was permitted to be happy in his quiet garden anticipating, as it were, before the "call came," something of the beatitude of the fairy paradise of his lifelong confidence.

STUDLAND

AT the beginning of the century, before the townsmen of Bournemouth were encouraged to invade Dorset, the village of Studland was almost without a rival for its unspoilt, old-fashioned beauty. The approach to the sea was most lovely. It was by way of a lane, typical West Country lane with high overgrown banks such as are commonly to be found in the Blackmore Vale. These damp high banks in the springtime would be covered with primroses and in and out of the undergrowth warblers would flutter foraging amongst the fresh leaves and buds for a particular diet, their quick preoccupied movements suggesting the near approach of the nesting season.

This quiet unassuming lane never for a moment betrayed its proximity to the sea, and yet when one reached its end there were the dancing waves, the waves of one's childhood dreams, bright and blue and restless against the white sails and white cliffs. On the horizon opposite across the wide level of these sunny waters stood out the Isle of Wight, its proud marble gate that gave entrance and egress to a world-wide traffic, clearly visible. To the right towered the Ballard Downs, bold in outline and terminating in a colossal fragment of chalk named by fishermen "The Haystack," a fragment of chalk that the envious ocean had detached from the formidable mass of those eternal hills and which it intends, in due time, to demolish entirely. To the left on the further side of a low sandy cliff was an inland sea and sand dunes and a moor stretching far away to the lagoons of Branksea Island.

Memories of Studland remain with me always—the gorse against the grass and sea and sky fringing the coast's edge with banks and heaps of gold, the insistent crying of the gulls about the Old Harry Rock louder than I have ever heard gulls cry since audible from the road to Swanage and lasting all through the soft April nights—the glimpse I got of some Dorset deer on the heath, suddenly present upon the crest of a sandy hillock, their branched heads poised for one suspended moment before a swift and noiseless flight away, away, away!

I came upon these mediæval animals a mile or so beyond the Agglestone Rock, a magnificent rock of ferruginous sandstone that has proved strong to resist the attrition of the determined centuries. Visitors to Dorset often question me about the odd-shaped stones they see hung up on the walls of our houses and I explain that no one of prudence in the county ever passes a stone with a hole through it with indifference, but is careful to preserve such fortunate fragments for the sake of the good luck they bring, fragments named by our Saxon ancestors Haligstan, and by us called Holy stones. Well instructed have we been from our childhood by the "superstitious, idle-headed eld" to venerate such toys of chance, whether they be so small that they can be hung upon a back-door nail red with rust, or like the Agglestone on Studland Common, of such enormous proportions that a whole cartload of devils, push and pull as they might, would be unable to budge it the breadth of a cherry-stone from its deep-rooted foundation.

Scotch firs flourish in the locality of Studland, and in August the air is often made light with the fresh health-giving odour that the warmth of an idle summer's afternoon can draw out of fallen pine needles. Three splendid hollies used also to grow not far from Littlesea Lake. In winter how their leaves would shine and how the hungry birds would gather about them! For years the second part of Matthew Arnold's poem, "Tristram and Iseult," has been associated in my mind with those romantic seaside hollies.

"In the smooth centre of the opening stood
Three hollies side by side and made a screen,
Warm with the winter-sun, of burnished green
With scarlet berries gemm'd, the fell-fare's food."

The longest walk of my life is connected with Studland. When we were boys I set out from Montacute with my brother Bertie to visit our brother Theodore who was then living in a cottage opposite the Post Office at Studland. Our bicycles broke down at Mappowder in the middle of Dorset, and arranging that they should be taken back to Yeovil by the carrier, we started on foot, "on Shank's Mare," to use an expression of the period, for the Island of Purbeck. We passed through Milton Abbas and Bere Regis and Wareham and Corfe Castle.

Was it perhaps the Frome itself by whose banks we rested bathing our tired feet? I have never been able to find again those shady water-meadows, though I have more than once gone over our route trying to do so, and though my memory of them remains clear. It was nearing to the end of the long summer's day and we sat side by side refreshing outselves by the waters of a crystal stream, a stream as transparent as glass that flowed above a floor of separate shining pebbles, a stream whose rich banks were thick grown with comfrey, meadow-sweet, and with purple loose-strife, a flower of somewhat rank habit to which "liberal shepherds give a grosser name, but our cold maids do dead man's fingers call." Except for the murmur of a distant wood-pigeon there was nothing to disturb the tranquillity of the sacred hour of evening unless it were abrupt intermittent splashing of a rising fish, the most cool, the most happy of sounds! This vanished halting place of my boyhood's memory was just such a By-Path Meadow as John Bunyan describes in *The Pilgrim's Progress*. "On either side of the river was also a meadow curiously beautified with lilies; and it was green all the year long . . . also here, as you see, are delicate waters, pleasant meadows, dainty flowers."

It was not till the small hours of the next morning that we came down the hill by the fir plantation to my brother's house. In those leisurely days it was a pleasure to walk along country roads at night. Motor-cars, inventions of Satan disastrous to every form of civilised life, were seldom if ever to be met with on the easy untarred turnpikes of the octogenarian Queen, and continually the untrimmed dusty hedges gave out for a traveller's refreshment warm puffs of the yellow honeysuckle's sweetest breath.

My father, though it was unlike him to do so, had expressed a wish that while I was away I would attend a church service

High West Street, Dorchester.

Chydyock: Llewelyn Powys' home, 1931–1936.

every Sunday, and on this account the Norman church of Studland, squat as a grey toad in a field of oblong emmet butts, became more familiar to me, with its stolid walls and subsiding chancel arch, than I could have anticipated or desired, but although by a scrupulous obedience I honoured my father's authority my own wayward inclination led me continually to the great Holy Stone on the open moorland. I remember visiting it after one of these Sunday evening services when a harvest moon, round and honey-coloured, was in the heavens. In those days I valued this ambiguous planet equally with the sun and would often find great liberation for my mind in meditating upon her wide sway. I knew that she was on that evening illuminating the free earth in every continent and climate, illuminating pyramids and temple gates, tusks of ivory and beaks of horn, the hair that covers the notched back-bones of animals and the hair that grows upon the scalps of men; even the criss-cross prickles of hedgehogs she was transforming into bodkins of purest silver by her bland and universal enchantment, the prickles of the sow hedge-pig occupied in edging herself towards the white dew-cold udder of a dairy cow which, with the simple dignity of her kind, would remain deep breathing and undisturbed while this lob of gipsy bacon was receiving its nourishment through the short calm hours of a summer's night in a far-off fairy valley by the banks of the River Frome.

GAY LEOPARDS

MY two eldest brothers had been visiting me in my open-air shelter at the end of the cottage garden, and just as they were leaving my brother John brought me in his hand a weasel which had been killed by my sister's cat. "Littleton," he observed, "thinks it is a stoat because there is so much white on its belly." I looked at the animal covered by its handsome russet pelt. It is of course a mistake to suppose the stoat can be differentiated from the weasel by the white fur that invests its throat, breast, belly, and the insides of its legs. The weasel, in proportion to its size, possesses just as much white as does its cousin. The two creatures are to be correctly distinguished in two ways; the stoat is larger than the weasel and it invariably carries at the end of its more prosperous tail a tuft of black hair.

Stoats and weasels are common on the Dorset Downs, so I have had many opportunities of observing them and their ways. The stoats feed mostly upon rabbits and the weasels on the mice and rats that collect about the cornstacks and lonely barns, though either of the animals is prepared to exchange its diet at a moment's notice. I have heard it said that the terror experienced by a hare when the beagles are after her is so great that some of the lighter bones in her body literally turn to water. The fear that a stoat inspires in the hearts of rabbits can be scarcely less intense.

For two or three years my shelter was placed near an ancient earthwork known in the district as the Pound. The earthwork is entirely overgrown with elder-trees, thorn-trees, and brambles, and it offers harbourage for wild life of every kind. I have seen foxes and hedgehogs emerge from its undergrowth, and it has always been a great hunting-ground for stoats and weasels. Some thirty yards from where my shelter stood there used to lie an old charred log half hidden by the foot-grass of the earthwork. Doubtless it marked the place of some fire by which farm labourers had sat in an interval of ploughing or threshing. On two occasions I saw a stoat deliberately rubbing its body against this log in order that its odour might arrest the attention of others of its kind passing that way, and the log would always preserve something of the familiar musky smell of these little beasts. I remember that one morning when this smell was particularly strong I heard a rabbit screaming a little distance in the field. I went to the place and it ran off in that haunted way characteristic of rabbits when they think a stoat is after them. There was no stoat anywhere to be seen and I believe a mere whiff of the fatal trysting log was alone sufficient to cause the meek-hearted grass eater to be overcome in a paroxysm of terror.

Not long ago I noticed some unfamiliar object on the ground near the garden gate of my cottage. I examined it with a pair of field-glasses and saw it was a full-grown rabbit lying on its side, indifferent to its danger from cat or dog, careless of its exposed position. It required a Dionysian heart to view with serenity this pitiable bundle of grey fur. I could see clearly the great staring brown eye, unblinking and panic-stricken, and the abdomen of the prostrate animal rising and falling at each breath that it took. Presently it struggled once more to its feet to continue its hopeless flight.

No carnivorous animals are more cunning or more resolute than are the stoat and the weasel. Their very gait betrays the sinister determination of their natures as they follow along in pursuit of their game with an infinite patience and an infinite confidence, pausing periodically to sniff the air with upraised heads.

One day last spring I heard a shocking cry come from the garden, the shrill hysterical cry of a creature beside itself with pain and vindictiveness. My sister's tabby-cat, apparently finding this particular dog-stoat too much of an undertaking, had dropped it wounded in the flower-bed, and the sound I heard came from the throat of this gay leopard outraged in its deepest pride.

These animals do not know what fear is. They will without hesitation enter the over-populated underground tenements of rats that an animal of better sense would avoid. What an electric psychic current must pass between a rat and one of these quadruped serpents when they suddenly confront each other in a darkened hole conjuring up with a single deadly glance imminent death—the rat with his untrustworthy physiognomy and hairless tail, the stoat with his appalling eyes illumined by a ghastly intention.

A mole is a favourite quarry for the weasel. Shepherds on these downs often show me dead weasels that have set off their mole traps. Weasels will follow moles to the furthest extremities of their tunnels. The moles themselves have voracious appetites and are for ever searching for worms and beetles. It must be a startling experience for one of them to be suddenly aware of the approach of an enemy, as with thick muscular wrists it is occupied with its solitary labours at the end of a pitch-dark passage.

How strange to meditate upon these underground tragedies! Is He who is rumoured to mark the fall of a common house-sparrow too hard of hearing to catch the smothered and desperate supplication of a mole in its arched and silent corridor? And does the weasel as she draws into her being the life-blood of her sturdy victim relish it less on her experienced palate than the blood of the common rat, or the heart's blood of a field-mouse, purer and perhaps less heady to the taste?

Bewick says that these creatures live by "cruelty" and rapine, and as always the old coffin-plate engraver does not shoot far from the mark—and yet what country scene is there that suggests a well-being more exultant than does a litter of weasels playing with their dam? There is no stint to their high spirits as they twirl and scamper, exercising their limber bodies in anticipation of their life's employment.

When my shelter was placed on the lee side of the Pound one of my greatest pleasures in the winter was to watch the slow breaking of the dawn. I would usually wake at six o'clock when night was still present and the stars were shining as if nothing would ever again dim their calm and steadfast influence; and then there would come a scarcely discernible lessening of the sky's density away towards the east, and soon afterwards the hoarse abrupt diluvian cry of the first hungry gull flying inland! This familiar cry of vigorous life voyaging under a zenith still bright with constellations would be followed by intermittent twitterings of the awakened small birds. There was a cock blackbird that used to roost in the topmost twigs of a leafless elder-tree only ten feet from my hut. It was the custom of this bird to spend several minutes preening its feathers in the half-light, before, with a succession of sharp screams of pretended panic, it flew noisily away over the hedge already barred with the fiery horizontal lines of the sunrise. One morning I caught a note of authentic panic in its cry and sitting up I observed a weasel balanced in the small branches of the elder, swaying its snake-like head backwards and forwards in chagrin at having missed the bird after so difficult a climb. A few minutes later the sun had risen above the horizon and the sensible matter-of-fact day made it seem almost incredible that I had been a witness to such an audacious example of crepuscular treachery.

In country places stoats and weasels are always associated with some kind of atrocity. The pluck of these vermin is their sole virtue and it is unsurpassed by any animal.

From a moral point of view the character of their blood relation, the badger, is on a far higher plane, for it combines the dauntless courage of their common ancestry with a disposition that is extremely amiable. This friendly, bear-like, blackberry-eating "great weasel" has, upon occasions, been observed contently sharing his roomy domicile with a fox, in spite of his own cleanly and dignified habits, out of sheer good nature being willing to put up with the ill conduct of so shiftless a comrade.

In ancient times old families were not only distinguished in heraldry by the possession of a crest, but by an hereditary badge as well. The lines of grey-white hair that are so conspicuous a feature of the badger's countenance may well be accepted as signifying the ancient claim of this honourable member of a large family to gentle blood. Indeed because of these very badges the name "badger" is more generally in use now than is the earlier name "brock"; though it may with profit be observed that under the ordinance of Nature the distinguishing markings of this nobler branch of the family are placed on the head, reserving for stoat and weasel the fitting edict of carrying ermine beneath jaw and belly.

STINSFORD CHURCHYARD

I REMEMBER once when Mr. Middleton Murry had driven over to White Nose from his house at Abbotsbury that our conversation turned to Mr. Thomas Hardy's long life. My roving mind hazarded a speculation as to what had been the earliest earth-memory retained in the great man's head. To my satisfaction I discovered that this scrap of information I had reckoned lost had actually been communicated to my visitor. It was a memory very simple and so essentially belonging to the universal heritage of human kind that it might have served equally well for the first memory of Confucius as for the first memory of King Alfred the Great.

The long stream of impressions, so powerful and so poetical, that were to follow each other through Mr. Hardy's mind for over eighty years, had their beginning, it seems, in the child's fascinated contemplation of the round shining belly of an enormous new kitchen kettle brought back from Dorchester market to the home at Upper Bockhampton by Mrs. Hardy's mother. It was just such a first memory as Homer would have delighted to put on record had he had occasion to write of the hours of Ulysses' infancy, sitting with his nurse Eurycleia. What a long span of decades was to pass, momentous for the thought and literature of England, between the hour when the child gazed with wonder at the shining cauldron, and the hour when the old man's heart, that morsel of "priceless dust," was buried in its silver casket under the Hardy yew-tree in Stinsford churchyard! And what a fitting parcel of ground it was for the burying of Hardy's heart—that heart which understood the mysterious affections of the hearts of girls better than any one since William Shakespeare's time. Here it lies surrounded close by the firm long-lasting bones of his sturdy ancestry.

There are few walks in Dorset more pleasant than the one that crosses Grey's Bridge and follows the footpath through

Stinsford water-meadows. How clear is the little watercress stream which, to use one of Mr. Hardy's own phrases, "crinkles" by at the bottom of Church Lane! That good man, Lord Sidney Godolphin Osborne, who at one time held the living of Durweston, near Blandford, tells us of churchyards so burdened and crowded with decayed men that they were abandoned by the very lobworms. This is not so at Stinsford. Here the dead are received with peace into the earth. To rest here on a sunshine spring morning among the celandines and long grasses is to be relieved of half the dread of execrable death. Surely there can be no great evil in a monarch whose wide scattered estate can include a plot so harmless, and so quiet.

How often must Thomas Hardy as a boy have walked along the river-side path shadowed by great trees leading from the bridge of Lower Bockhampton; running before his parents, perhaps, to see the fish dart into hiding beneath the green floating water-weeds, or marking from a gap in the hedge a crested patient heron keeping hungry watch over a shallow dike on the further side of the field. Nearly three miles must separate Stinsford Church from Thomas Hardy's birthplace at Upper Bockhampton. And what a dwelling this old house was! A large thatched cottage standing in its own grounds at the end of a blind lane, and beyond it the heather stretching away to Puddletown, to Moreton, to Studland!

I have been told that Mr. Hardy used to read at the upstairs window removed furthest from the little wicket-gate that gave entrance to his father's property. There must remain even now many branches of the fine trees in the woodland opposite that have scarce altered their shape since those days, so poorly does the longest life of frail man compare with the leisurely longevity of mute timber.

One of Mr. Hardy's relations, an old gentleman of over eighty, himself a poet of considerable local celebrity, has described to me how dear the heath was to his famous cousin in the days of his youth, and how there used to be a huge monolith standing in the bracken not far from the Hardy home, and how Thomas Hardy used to love the stone, often loitering by it, and how it was in the end broken up by some practical-minded rascal envious of such good material for road making.

This section of Egdon heath, of King Lear's heath, has an extraordinary attraction quite apart from its intimate associations with the personality of the greatest poet of our age. The bracken here is so tall that lovers on their Sunday walks need never be disturbed by anything worse than mid-summer flies.

How delightful to leave the moor with its fir-tree spinnies, its clumps of goblin German-like forests, and go down to the rich meadows of the Frome. The water forget-me-nots growing at the river's edge are the largest I have ever seen. They resemble the blue eyes of children who, unlearned in betrayals, look innocently up at you and who never will forget! The juxtaposition of the lean, scraggy moorlands with those fat fields below could not have failed to impress Mr. Hardy's boyhood imagination. On many an early summer morning he must have seen the milkmaids cross the meadows rendered mysterious by the gossamer mists of a West Country night, have marked them like so many Tess d'Urbervilles, pails and milking-stools in hand, leaving behind them at every step a track of scattered dew.

I remember one hot summer afternoon bathing in the lovely river, so glass-clear, so utterly different in smell and appearance from the sluggish waters of the Yeo, the Parrett, the Stour. Coming away from my hidden pool I had to pass through a clover field which was being "fed off" by hurdled sheep. The shepherd who had the flock under his care, was an elderly man with a typical Dorset countenance and a splendid ashen crook. Once when I was at Max Gate I had admired very much a small oil-painting of just such a weather-beaten shepherd. Mrs. Hardy told me that Mr. Hardy was so fond of it that he had always had it hanging near his bed. May not perhaps the small dim picture have been among the last objects that Mr. Hardy's eyes rested upon, bringing to his mind this most primitive of all human occupations, associated for most of us with Biblical symbolism? So that the poet's final earth-memory may well have had to do with old scenes of penned ewes in fields of winter roots in the lowlands around Bockhampton, or with the fairy music of sheep bells on the far away sky-line uplands of his beloved downs.

"Round about me bulged the barrows
As before, in antique silence—immemorial funeral piles—
Where the sleek flocks trampled daily the remains of flint-tipt arrows
'Mid the thyme and chamomiles."

THE RIVER YEO

THOUGH the whole length of the River Yeo's course does not amount to many miles, its most extensive stretches belong to Somerset. Its chief source, however, is to be found a little above Sherborne Lake, near the Poyntington road, in the county of Dorset. The river has not been used too well in recent years by the townsfolk of Sherborne, but fortunately, through the blessed purifications of nature, it is still able to refresh the wide beautiful goose plains of Lenthay Common. From Lenthay the Yeo flows to Bradford Abbas, eventually reaching Yeovil through the Park of Newton House, and later meandering slowly on through the fat low country of Somerset, until, a mile above Langport, it joins with the River Parrett. Its actual source is known as "the Seven Sisters." A considerable distance intervenes between these springs and the ornamental eighteenth century bridge which stands at the further end of Sherborne Lake. This bridge is an English type of those pleasure-garden bridges of the Chinese such as beguile our fancy on old-fashioned ware. I could, however, scarcely imagine a more English scene than is presented to a wayfarer who loiters here on a mid-summer afternoon—a scene more secure, more blandly tranquil, with the dappled fallow deer grazing lightly on the sunshine lawns of the park, with cuckoos calling from the trees in all directions, and with buttercup fields decked with brightest gold. I do not suppose the turf of these slopes has ever known a period when it has been unpressed by the delicate pointed hoofs of deer. Wild stags of some kind or another must have been snuffing at the air and gracefully tossing their antlered heads under the great trees of Selwood Forest even from Neolithic times.

How well I remember as a little boy being conducted by our tall schoolmaster, W. H. Blake, to look over the ruins of Sherborne Castle! This old Tory schoolmaster from Norfolk was, indeed, more of a country gentleman than a pedagogue, but for all that he had a gift for stirring our imaginations with a sense of past history. There was in his hall at Acreman House a stuffed pike, the largest I have ever seen, which he had caught in Sherborne Lake with a spinning spoon of his own devising. We little boys, in our white collars and Eton jackets, used to contemplate its ichthyoid countenance with wide-eyed wonder, the ferocious physiognomy, with sulky under-jaw, of this huge legless creature large enough to eat any of us up; which must have been the dreaded dictator of some dark water-lily abyss, sharking after, and devouring wholesale, I know not how many small fry, year after year, between Lady Day and Michaelmas!

The lake would often freeze in the Easter term and the school and town would come in Shrove Tuesday troops to disport themselves. The ice would be as smooth as horn and very black, and while the bigger boys, wearing their velvet football caps, joined in well organised games of hockey, the rest of us would cruise about the pond's edge trying to keep warm. Meanwhile, far up above our heads, and the heads of the light-heeled crowd, carrion crows, intimidated into silence by the cold, would fly across the sky in the direction of Alexander Pope's "forest" on Jerusalem Hill.

In the summer time, when the chestnut trees are all in flower, Sherborne used to seem a city most soothing to the senses—always the eyes fell upon tender, living leaves spreading themselves out against grey stones articulate with memories of a forgotten age. If Weymouth is the most beautiful of all Dorset towns in August when a thousand children dance upon its sands; and Dorchester most to be praised at Christmas when the town pavements are crowded with people come in from the country; and Bridport most to be admired in April when its solid burgomasters accidentally raising their eyes, as the advance down this broad flax-retting main street, become suddenly aware that the distant hills rising to view at the west end of the town have changed over night to a fresh parrot-back green; then Sherborne in the early summer is without doubt "the flour of Cities all" in Dorset. Of it Leland writes: "The towne of Sherborne standith partely on the brow of an hill partely in a botom. I esteme it to lak litle of a two miles in cumpace. For a dry town or other, saving Pole that is a little thing, I take it to be the best towne at this present tyme in Dorsetshire."

Sherborne takes its names from the Yeo, being derived from the words "scir burne," meaning clear stream. Yet how turgid the river can become during the winter months after heavy rains, as cold and chill it whirls past the leafless willow trees, sweeping violently round each mud-shelving grass-over-lapping bend! What a sense of desolation it can then evoke, with small birds in dull-coloured feathers moving disconsolately amongst grey broken water-washed reeds, by the side of a grey drowning torrent, under grey clouds.

The sedge is wither'd from the lake
And no birds sing.

Again, what a transmutation in the summer! I have always remembered, as in a vision, a particular afternoon when I walked behind my older brother, Bertie, and one of his school friends named Blackborne. My Sunday top-hat was in my hand and I kept munching at the leaves of the tall red sorrel as the three of us sauntered through the paradise pastures beyond the Lenthay wood. My brother and Blackborne were the two cleverest boys in "Charlie Hodson's form," and during this walk our companion, a boy of remarkable charm, was gaily deprecating his chance of winning the form prize at the end of the term. Perhaps that particular Sunday afternoon stayed in my memory because during the next holidays my brother's unlucky friend was drowned while punting on the Thames.

Thirty years afterwards I happened to meet in New York a lace merchant, a gallant old gentleman with a curled pate and a courtesy of manner suggesting the period of the Regency. Recognising at once that he was an Englishman I entered into conversation with him. He was Blackborne's father. I remained reticent—for how could I hope to convey to the imagination of this quaint old trafficker the clearness with which I recalled walking by the side of the very boy for whom, as he confided to me, he had never ceased to mourn, walking by his side in what seemed to me a mirage world, quivering with yellow sunshine and hayfield grasses by the idle waters of the River Yeo?

LYME REGIS

THE coast-line of the county of Dorset is guarded on its eastern and western extremities by two sturdy towns, Poole and Lyme Regis, which have always been as truculent as they are ancient. Few who have attempted to meddle with their liberties have done so with impunity. They are far-famed for their breed of honest seamen with a smack of the land about them—trawling fishermen, who can make themselves handy in a hay-field, and yet for all that they can use a pick well, can pull at an oar better. During the Civil War both Poole and Lyme Regis were brisk for the cause of Parliament, and an historian of those times reports that when Prince Maurice had reduced all the rest of Dorset these two small towns "returned so peremptory a refusal to the Prince's summons that his Highness resolved not to attack them."

Perhaps it is the Cobb, the extraordinary Breakwater of the royal city of Lyme Regis, that helps to give to the place its idiosyncratic character. If you look down upon this old structure from the hills above, it takes on the appearance of a vole's flat tail left dangling on the water outside its slippery retreat. The old monosyllabic word Cobb in mediæval times had many uses. A male herring was called a Cobb, a black-backed gull, a miller's thumb; and with no great stretch of the imagination the Breakwater to-day may in truth be thought to resemble the king digit of the miller's "cluster o' vive." It is probable, however, that this odd barricade against the Channel waves earned its name from actually being "a rounded heap of stones." The Cobb was first built in the reign of Edward I, and it is likely enough that it would be possible to find at sea level in its marrowbone, so to speak, massy rocks whose fate has been as uneventful and unchanged as has that of the "stolen stone" of Longshanks over which seven hundred dusty centuries have passed in Westminster Abbey as it were in a day.

With the Cobb on one side, the church on the other, and with its principal thoroughfare winding sideways down from the high hill behind, a very compact and solid seaside town is presented to the traveller who is exploring for the first time this furthermost corner of Dorset. There still exist in Lyme Regis small bow-windows against the panes of which, during the stormy months of autumn, quiet Victorian ladies may be seen standing to draw their thick winter curtains; while in the sweet months of spring and summer these same rounded bottle-glass partitions present to the passer-by the angel faces of idle children, bright with seaside sunshine.

When Tennyson visited Lyme Regis people were eager to show him the place where Monmouth landed. "Don't talk to me of the Duke of Monmouth," he said impatiently. "Show me the exact spot where Louisa Musgrove fell!" I have never thought much of this anecdote. The poet was putting too high a value upon the craft of imaginative fiction. The interest to be attached to the phantoms of literary invention can never be compared to that which belongs to men and women who have actually lived, even though, as in this case, the hero of the piece was but a sorry Prince, with cosmetics in his silken fob, the bastard child of "bold brown Lucy Walters."

On several occasions my father elected to visit Lyme Regis for his yearly holiday, travelling from Montacute by train to Axminster, and then conveying us all in a carriage and pair to a row of houses at the extreme west of the town, a row called Ozone Terrace, a name that never failed to charm and amuse my mother. Ozone Terrace was happily situated for us children. We soon discovered that these houses stood close to "The Landslide," a wild "forest" far more interesting to us than was the Cobb even with its harbour and custom house. This undercliff—rough, rocky, and luxuriant—extends westward almost as far as Seaton. For centuries the coast-line must have been disordered here, but the natural chaos of its outline was accentuated beyond imagination in the year 1840, when no less than fifty acres of good farm land slid down.

We used to call this borderland to Lyme Regis "the Fairy Glade"—and no wonder! It included a hundred dells with secret silent lawns surrounded by rankest undergrowth. In such places Ariel, that "tricksie sprite," might have been set to serve the term of his second punishment, crying out "as fast as mill-wheels strike," pegged tight, as Prospero had threatened, in the "knotty entrails" of an oak. Nor would anyone be surprised to come upon Miranda and Caliban standing close, the tender girl out of a pure benevolence trying to teach the blinking eyes of the hairy monster to distinguish a man, a dog, and a lantern in the shadows of the harvest moon. Sir George Somers, who was wrecked on the "still-vexed Bermoothes," and from the tales of whose adventures many of the ideas of *The Tempest* are derived, was himself born at Lyme Regis. I have never been to Bermuda, but I have seen certain coast-lines in the West Indies that in their physical features resemble closely "The Landslide" of Lyme Regis, though the flora, of course, is entirely different. In the spring the hawthorn-trees of this Dorset wilderness can hardly be matched anywhere else in England, acres upon acres of embossed and garlanded May flowers, their rich smell, redolent of a careless happy sensuality, for a few fugitive days making the surrounding air heavy with delight—so soon, soon, lost in the noiseless scattering of a myriad unnoticed petals, white and round.

At one time during the Great War it was the occupation of my brother Willie to collect cattle in the Congo and trek them down to depots of the British troops then serving in German East Africa. Besides the natives he had one white man with him, a Dorset man whose employment it had been in the fat days of peace to drive "holiday fools" to and fro between Axminster and Lyme Regis. During the long equatorial nights my brother would often read out of his copy of William Barnes's poems, so that both he and his companion might be reminded of their homes; and sometimes this "jolly postboy" would while away the time by describing to my brother the exact habits of a great grey gelding which throughout the 'nineties had munched oats, damp and dry, in the stables of the Black Dog; or sometimes by recounting to him stories of afternoons spent with buxom nursemaids tumbling in the bracken of the Fairy Glade at that time of the year when the white flowers of the privet had turned rusty red, and the lower bells of the fox-gloves were already lost, and late summer flies were everywhere murmuring in the patched sunshine. Then with their heads full of old Dorset memories they would lie side by side until waked by the punctual crowing of my brother's farmyard cock, his heart's delight, which he carried along with him on all his journeys through forest and plain, and which on fine nights would invariably settle itself to roost on the spear of the tent-pole as though trying to simulate the brass vane on the top of St. Catherine's Church at Montacute.

Lyme Regis at one time was a great place for fishing, but now, save for a little "potting," few men go out. From White Nose on any day when the visibility was average I used to be able to see beyond Lyme Regis to the chalk cliffs of Beer, and it is from this Devonshire village, and from Sidmouth still further to the west, that most of the fishing in this quarter of the Bay is done. The Sidmouth fishermen and the Lympstone men, or "stumpy-tail hookers" as they are nicknamed, often take "their marks" from Rousdon—that is to say, locate their exact position on a fishing bed by getting this far-seen landmark above "The Landslide" of Lyme Regis in exact line with some nearer "sight." "Thousand-in-Bush and Rousdon," Bob Wooley might shout across the waves to Tom. It is an odd fact that many of these "marks" that are every day upon the lips of the fishing brotherhood would mean nothing to the landsman if he heard them alluded to in conversation. A particularly conspicuous field from the sea may earn itself a name such as "Thousand-in-Bush" and perhaps be known as "honey-plot" by the labourer who for more than half a century has been turning over its tilth at the plough's tail.

The occupations of the inhabitants of Lyme have been various. In the year seven hundred and seventy-four Cenwulf granted land to certain men whose office it became to boil salt out of sea-water for use in the butteries and kitchens of Sherborne Abbey. In Queen Elizabeth's days the shipping that sheltered in the lew of the Cobb was, it is said, "one-sixth that of London." Later the manufacture of serge cloth flourished here. When I was a boy there were lime-kilns on the shore beyond Ozone Terrace. New fashions, new houses, have largely marred the simple dignity of this old Dorset town; only the Cobb has been found firm to resist every change, still obstinately fulfilling the primitive task for which it was built.

WEYMOUTH IN THE THREE EIGHTS

WHEN I was a child there used to be a great excitement if a seagull flew over the garden of our home in Somerset. We were accustomed to cock-pheasants, rooks, blackbirds, and fly-catchers, but not to these hungry birds of the winds and waves. Far up above the acacia, above the lawns and sunny flower-beds, they would pass with deliberate purpose on their way back to the sea.

In those days we children knew of only one sea—Weymouth Bay! Clearly I remember how it first suddenly appeared to me as I came up King Street—a wide field of bright-blue water under a curved and cloudless sky. My grandmother lived in a brick house at the further end of Brunswick Terrace, and while my mother, together with "the little ones" and the luggage, was being conveyed there in the old horse-drawn bus of the Burdon Hotel, I had been allowed to walk along the front with my nurse Emily Clare.

A peculiar glamour hangs over my memories of Weymouth in the year 1888. There must have been many inhabitants living then in the royal watering-place who remembered the battle of Waterloo; and truly the look of the "Boscawen," and the look of the huge frigates, their bulging white sails so often visible on the horizon, could not help suggesting to an imaginative mind the Dorset of Captain Hardy and King George III!

To leave the seclusion of Montacute to come to Weymouth was to feel oneself surrounded by the romance of English history. The man who brought buckets of sea water to Penn House every morning had been, so we were always told, a great favourite with our Uncle Littleton, a soldier who had died in India before I was born. This water-carrier had an iron hook in place of the hand which he had lost in battle. What a sight it was on Sundays, standing at the window below the venetian blinds which smelt of sunshine and seaside dust, to watch the after-church procession pass along the Esplanade; the redcoats with their swaggering gallantry who were, so I liked to imagine, part of the garrison of the Nothe, of the Nothe that in my eyes was the most perfect model of all forts, with a real portcullis, and real sentries, and real iron cannons of the Napoleon wars; while everywhere interspersed amongst the soldiers with their pouting red chests, would-be blue-jackets, easy, free, and loose-limbed as cats, idling after the girls. This was before the Esplanade had been disfigured by modern utilitarian shelters, when the street and the parade were separated by a looped chain suspended from a succession of squat monoliths of Portland stone, which in the morning sunshine as I went by them with spade and bucket, would gleam with dazzling seaside whiteness.

Life was less efficient in those days, but surely it passed more pleasantly. It held for me many mysteries, some of which even now continue to perplex my mind. How, for instance, was it possible for the common earth above St. John's Gardens to conceal real crystals, veritable moonstones fit to be set in silver? When my father first initiated me into this unsuspected secret I was amazed, and to this day when I look out of the East Chaldon carrier's van at the smart villas now built upon this treasure site of my childhood I can hardly trust my memory. It was also the custom of my father to bring back from Portland, that far-distant island, well-selected round flat pebbles far larger than any I had ever seen and on which it was my grandmother's delight to paint pictures of Stalbridge Cross and the Lake of Geneva! Then there were the cowries I used to find, tiny cowries smooth as ivory, with my new playmate, Kitty Steel, the sight of whom at the end of the terrace would set my infant's heart fluttering, so early did I seem to appreciate the sweet symbolism of our spindrift trophies.

In my child's mind the sea front was always separated into two strict divisions. To the right as I came out of the door was all the gaiety of a Vanity Fair, with varnished pleasure boats, entertainment shows, fairy-story goat-carriages, and white flat happy sands good for building castles. To the left was a more sombre expanse where the sea was rough and had to be kept by banks of heavy pebbles from breaking over into Lodmoor, that wild waste of bird-haunted marshland. It was upon the top of these great beaches to the more serious east that real fishing-boats were stabled, true deep-sea fishing-boats hollow and benched. Near them I had once seen a draught of fishes brought to land in an encircling net buoyed with corks and strained to breaking-point, a harvest of silver light leaping against the stout black mesh, just as the fish were represented as doing in the Bible picture-book kept in the Sunday cupboard at home.

It was on the other side of the old Red Post, which for many years marked the place where bathing from the beach was allowed, that my father took me one morning to bathe. The importance of wetting my head against the sun's heat had already been impressed upon me and as I walked by my father's side along the sea-path, for in those days the Esplanade did not extend to Greenhill Terrace, I resolved to obey this inexorable mandate by voluntarily lying prostrate at the water's edge until some harmless wave such as I was looking at would wash over me without violence. Alas! When all was ready and I stood prepared to put my plan into action I simply could not do it. The sea seemed so cold, so large, so strong. My father observed my hesitation, and, lifting me into his arms began like a Gulliver, or a benevolent Giant Grumble, to stride forward into the deeper water that separated the shore from "the first sandbank." When the waves were as high as his chest he deliberately lowered his arms until I was entirely submerged. This "ducking" was so terrifying to me that I swallowed an incredible amount of salt water and in consequence was violently sick. It was now my father's turn to feel alarm, and in a very little time I was being carried with tender concern back to my mother. An inhibition about any form of "ducking" has remained with me ever since. At Sherborne I learned to swim, but never to dive, and even now I seldom fail to hold my nose and shut my mouth tight before putting my head under water.

One day I was taken by Emily to ride a donkey. This had been a great ambition with me. All went well in spite of the unexpected jolting. A barefooted nut-brown boy ran at my side. We had gone in the direction of the pier where there were not so many people. I found difficulty in turning the donkey and on one of these occasions my companion who was older than I tugged fiercely at the bridle, in doing which he broke a strap. "You will be put in gaol for this," he said, adding significantly: "You wait till I tell Masser." I immediately appreciated the predicament I was in. With such a consummate liar as sole witness of what had happened I was convinced that the liberty of my person was in grave jeopardy. I was only four years old, but already an infant Ulysses, I had learned to "contrive in my heart," so that as soon as ever we returned to the stand, before the boy had had a chance to speak his winged words, I had slipped off the back of my ass, hurried on to the Esplanade, and in a trice edged myself into the very centre of a crowd that was engaged in watching a Punch-and-Judy show. All that afternoon a distracted search was made for me, but it was not until well on in the evening that I judged it prudent to begin sauntering back to Brunswick Terrace.

My grandmother* was a fragile old lady of eighty. She used to lie in a great bed that looked out over the sea, a delicate and brittle doll, her unwrinkled cheeks lightly flushed with a faint pink colour such as is to be seen sometimes on the inside surface of a shell. When I was taken to visit her she would show me pictures. On these occasions I would be placed on her bed. Her frilled pillows always smelt of rosewater and dried lavender. She would show me albums of old-fashioned frosted Christmas cards and faint water-colour sketches of the white cliffs she could see from her window stretching away as far as St. Aldhelm's Head.

It is hard for the mind of a child to accommodate itself to the austere ordinance by which all things are determined. My mother used to teach me that if I had sufficient faith my prayers could move mountains, and every morning and evening for many weeks I remember supplicating my father's God to make my grandmother so strong and well that she would be able to carry me pick-a-back across the "ante-room." It was an

* She was the wife of Rev. L. C. Powys, for many years the Rector of Stalbridge, Dorset.

innocent confidence, but not any more innocent perhaps than the happy beliefs entertained by this old lady who, when the rising moon shone bright upon Weymouth Bay, would often declare that its path was paved with sheets of gold in preparation for her journey to Heaven.

THE END